SALES TALES

True Stories of How Great Sales Happen

CONOR KENNY

Published by OAK TREE PRESS
19 Rutland Street, Cork, Ireland
www.oaktreepress.com / www.SuccessStore.com

© 2014 Conor Kenny

A catalogue record of this book is available from the British Library.

ISBN 978 1 78119 146 0 (Hardback)
ISBN 978 1 78119 147 7 (Paperback)
ISBN 978 1 78119 148 4 (ePub)
ISBN 978 1 78119 149 1 (Kindle)

CONTENTS

INTRODUCTION

In the mid-1970s, I was a schoolboy. My Dad had spent most of his career dreaming of owning a boat, a boat that had character and could sail away on the River Shannon. Eventually, he made his dream come true which, with five schoolgoing children, was some feat.

The *Saide R* was built in the 1940s and was a beautiful, elegant, timber cruiser. Its portholes were solid brass and she cut quite a dash heading down the Grand Canal, before running free on the Shannon.

Just before joining Ireland's longest river, we stopped at the last canal stop. Shannon Harbour was dominated by a derelict hotel, a relic of a bygone era of barges and trade. There wasn't much happening that evening in this very sleepy village. Excited by a new stop, I asked Dad if there was a chip shop in Shannon Harbour. He laughed and said: *"There are no chips in Shannon Harbour – but wouldn't that be a great title for a book?"*.

I always said that, if ever I wrote a book, I'd call it *No Chips in Shannon Harbour*. At least I got the title into the first few lines!

For the last 30 years, I have had some success and have made huge mistakes in selling. I have learnt by trial and error and, most of all, I have worked hard to understand what inspires a reaction and what makes people zone out. *Sales Tales* is based on my personal experiences and real encounters in pursuit of sales excellence.

Its purpose is to tell you some real-life stories that, I hope, you will relate to. It is not prescriptive and does not tell you what is right and what is wrong. On the contrary, it is descriptive and each story is underpinned by a powerful lesson that helped me the next time around.

My sales journey started when I was at university. I was a rather lazy student, who often thought I could 'think' my way to a fortune. I found academic theory difficult to translate into practice. It was interesting but

I wasn't always able to remember the complex analysis. To improve my own knowledge, I scoured bookshops for titles that I could understand. Of course, clever marketing people knew this and had their solution lying in wait.

I saw a book that promised to make my subject simple. It was a good book, a practical book and well-written too. It didn't really make the complex and abstract subject simple but it did teach me a powerful sales lesson that launched a deeper desire to understand the art of selling.

The colours had grabbed my attention. It was bigger than its competitors and stood fatter and higher than its skinny peers. It was confident, loud and clear. But, most importantly, the title had already made its mark. It was a promise – and it worked.

In the early 1990s, I worked for a particularly kind Jewish family in London. Arnold, the family head, was wise, successful and wealthy.

I had made a costly mistake in my youthful eagerness to sell. I was to meet Arnold the next morning. I felt like a man in the condemned cell.

The next day, in his office, I was nervous and feared the worst.

But, in his soft voice, Arnold said: "Conor, good decisions come from wisdom; wisdom comes from experience; experience comes from bad decisions".

That is how we learn – how we really learn. Sometimes, to believe the fire is hot, you need to get burnt. *Sales Tales* is based on my own occasional mis-steps into the fire. It is a book of real stories – sales stories that will teach you how to sell more. Here's to 'understanding' the fine art of how to be a much better sales person and to making more sales.

Conor Kenny
March 2014

CHAPTER 1
WHO ARE YOU?

Be yourself; everyone else is already taken.
Oscar Wilde

What are the skills that are fundamental to great sales?

There are many and, despite what many experts offer, there is no ultimate list or textbook to guide you. That would be too simplistic and would negate the complex web of skill required.

Of course, everything starts with our own inner self, our consciousness, who we are. It's important to be who you are and to be happy with who you are. If not, we run the terrible risk of being controlled by our ego. Some sales people are driven by ego. When they are, they are doomed to an unhappy end.

But what is this thing called ego? It's worth a little time to understand it. Here's what Eckhart Tolle says in his book, *A New Earth*:

> *Vanity and pride are what most of us tend to think of when we think of ego, but ego is much more than an overinflated sense of self. It can also turn up in feelings of inferiority or self-hatred because ego is any image you have of yourself that gives you a sense of identity – and that identity derives from the things you tell yourself and the things other people have been saying about you that you've decided to accept as truth.*

Understanding who you are is a critical step to understanding what you ought to do. To be simplistic about it, if you are not driven by ego and still curious about sales and perhaps the practicalities of a life selling, then the chances are that sales are for you.

And before you start, above all else, to thy own self be true.

❖

Let me tell you about three men I met at different points in my career. Each taught me a precious lesson. Each is very different, though they share one thing in common: they do what they want to do – but that certainly was not always the case.

But before you read their stories, think on a provocative lesson my Dad told me not so long ago.

There's No Such Thing as a Lazy Person

Ivor Kenny spent a lifetime working with managers. He is also a best-selling author and I'm lucky enough to call him Dad. One of his books – *Can You Manage?* – continues to teach and inspire many of our own students today. It's a powerful read.

One day, we were to receive a master class in management from Ivor. Like every good workshop, one lesson stood out above all the other rich pickings.

Ivor said, "There is no such thing as a lazy person". He paused and soaked up our incredulity.

"Yeah, right", we said quietly.

I knew my Dad better. There would be more.

There was.

"They are either sick or in the wrong job."

Instinctively, I disagreed. I could think of her, I could think of him, I could think of them. I thought a little longer. Like the light dawning, I began to see the absolutely obvious truth in Ivor's simple statement.

I had been there. I had hated my job. I had done everything in my bewildered power to avoid the job, my boss, the company and the customer. If you met me, I was lethargic, dull and disinterested. There was no energy, bounce or enthusiasm. I just did not care.

My shocking performance meant I was summoned to a solemn meeting. I walked the narrow corridor to meet the three judges. I still did not care. I wanted them to try me, find me guilty and announce my execution. They didn't. Instead, being good people, they tried to inspire me, motivate me and excite me.

They couldn't. Leaving their office without my execution date was a fate worse than death.

It took me a while – but then I realised *I* was the problem. I was in the wrong job. It's easy to see the symptoms, not so easy to see the cause. But, if, like I was, you're in the wrong job, you cannot succeed.

A few years afterwards, I suggested to my dad that he add a word to his diagnosis. It now runs: *"There's no such thing as a lazy person. They are either sick, lost or in the wrong job"*.

I know. I was lost once too.

The Three Wise Men

Sean

Sean was a really lovely chap. Considerate, quiet and gentle. Somehow, Sean got a job selling products that he should never have been selling. In fact, Sean was never cut out to be a salesman.

With a heavy heart, I was dispatched to end his miserable time with the company. We had always got on well. Sean had no idea that his end was near. We chatted and chatted and I couldn't find the words to begin the deadly deed. Eventually, I brought the conversation around to interests and passions.

Sean lit up. Excitedly, Sean talked horticulture. He couldn't speak fast enough. Passionate and deeply engrossed in his subject, Sean was oblivious to everything else – including questioning why we were meeting.

When the excitement ebbed, I asked Sean how he felt about where he worked.

"I just don't like it", he said instinctively.

I resisted the urge to probe more. Instead, I listened.

"You know, Conor, I think I'm in the wrong job. This is not my passion, not what I care about and not what I want."

I continued to listen.

"Conor, I've always enjoyed working with you. You have been good to me but I think I need to look out for myself a little more."

I nodded silently.

"This may be the wrong time, but it feels right. Conor, I'm so sorry, and I know you'll understand no matter how inconvenient, but I need to go. I need to leave. I need to follow my dreams. This is not my dream."

Sean left the next day. He never knew the executioner's rope had been coiled under the desk. It was a very happy ending.

Almost a year to the day, I got a call from a very happy man. It was Sean. He had started his own horticulture business and it was thriving. Sean had found his way.

Clifford

Cliff was my boss in London. He was a small man who always wore finely-cut Savile Row suits. He was a true English gentleman: beautiful manners, patient, gentlemanly and always dapper. I admired him and learnt a lot from simply observing him. I was very fond of my dandy boss.

One day, out of the blue, Cliff told me he was leaving the company. I assumed he was off to bigger greener pastures. I asked him where he was going.

He replied, "To a castle in Scotland that's in need of repair".

I was utterly perplexed.

Seeing my confusion, Cliff went on to explain: "You see, Conor, I turned 50 last month. I had always promised myself two careers – two very different careers. For the last 30 years, I have sold desks. Now, I'm going to rebuild this small castle and run it with my wife as a Bed & Breakfast. You only live once, Conor, and I'd rather have two careers than one".

It took me 20 years to 'get it' – but I did.

Gerry

Gerry was an ordinary guy. Ordinary-looking, ordinary at school. A nice guy but ordinary.

Gerry sat near me in mathematics class. Not my *forte* then and definitely not Gerry's. The teacher knew this but, because he seemed to like me, I was not the target of his verbal missiles – at least not too often.

This particular day, Gerry was caught unprepared for a difficult question on theorems. He walked to the front of the class to explain something he didn't know. An eternity later, humiliated, he walked slowly back to his seat, blushing an unhealthy shade of red. The teacher finished the onslaught by telling Gerry there was no point in him finishing school, since he would be lucky if he even made a meagre living as a tradesman.

Years later, as a frustrated law student who revelled in the theatre of the court room and persuasion, I used to dodge lectures in pursuit of court room drama. I'd hop on the bus and enter the Four Courts, enquiring excitedly as to what trial was where. Naturally, the bigger the offence, the more I wanted to watch.

It was a particularly nasty crime. It had murder and it had mystery. It was intriguing and the nation was watching. It was as high profile as they come. I sat watching the dramatic final moments and I marvelled at the oratory and the persuasion. For me, it was an open and shut case. The closing speech by the incredibly able, sharp and eloquent lawyer turned everyone's thinking, including the jury's. He saw things we didn't see. He created doubt where there was none and he was reasonable to a fault. He won his case. I was transfixed at the skill, the strategy and the power of his well-crafted words. It had been an interesting day.

Shortly after, I was in the main hall. A swift slap on my shoulder spun me around into the wig-wearing man in the trailing black gown. It was none other than my old school friend, Gerry.

Gerry, who had just won his case. Gerry, who I hadn't recognised because of his wig and gown. I was astonished but I was also delighted. Gerry had become one of the most successful barristers in the country.

We went for a quick coffee. I reflected on that awful day in school but resolved not to mention it. I didn't need to; he did: "Not bad for a young chap who was told to quit school and become a plumber, eh, Conor?".

Not bad, not bad at all.

CHAPTER 2
YOU CAN DO ANYTHING YOU WANT

It is not in the stars to hold our destiny but in ourselves.
William Shakespeare

It's a funny thing but, more often than not, people will avoid telling you they are in sales. They might be ambassadors, representatives, executives or 'in marketing'. It's as if 'sales' is a slightly tarnished word. It's not, nor should it ever be seen that way.

There is no service, no profession, no industry and no business that does not require sales, salesmanship and a sales strategy. Sales is a function that belongs to everyone, though it is one that many people shy away from. It is at the very core of strategy, every vision and every plan. It's a skill. And, when you see how common 'average' is, you can build a fantastic career by being in sales.

There's a huge difference between:

- What you can do;
- What you ought to do; and
- What you want to do.

The first often comes from a belief that our paths need to be sequential. In other words, because you've been in the automobile industry, you must stay in the automobile industry. That's a trap that exists only in your own mind.

The second is frequently the inheritance or legacy from an overpowering parent or guardian. It's their vision for you and, in some cases, might reflect a second surrogate shot at the career they never had. It's a dangerous path that often leads to failure.

The third is the only true option. What you want to do is pure, about you and your natural direction. If you listen to the inner instincts and let your compass guide you, you will succeed and prosper. Sales is not for everyone and it is a mistake to waste your time on undesirable pursuits.

As a student of philosophy and an avid reader of psychology, I am deeply interested in why we do what we do and the choices we make. From a very young age, I questioned everything. I had a deep desire to understand, not just know. I often questioned what I did and why I did it. Did I like it? Love it? Or did I just end up there? I was never too sure. This curiosity led me to an early career in selling, where that curiosity is essential.

One day, some deep reading led me to a very simple understanding, inspired by Eckhart Tolle, author of *The Power of Now*. Put simply (even simplistically), 'your story' is not 'who you are'. It's not easy to grasp at first but let me tell you why this is relevant.

We often believe our story or, if you like, our journey to here means we have to continue on. We don't. Your journey is your story but your journey is not who you are.

Before you go any further in a sales career, bear this in mind: your previous career does not mean it is your future path – you can change it. You can change it any time. You can change it many times. I know, I did.

What matters is that you are who you are, that you follow your innate passion – then success will follow. The story got you to here, to now, but that's all. From here on, you have choices. You are here but that does not mean you must stay here. If you do, and especially if you don't really want to, that's sequential thinking.

Sequential Thinking

I was caught in a trap. I had been living in London for the past nine years and I hated it. I couldn't see a way out. *"I have a mortgage, a car, a job. I have bills, I have direct debits and I'm a member of this and that"*. My head resembled a tumble-dryer. I was lost and trapped by my own thinking.

By chance, I ended up having dinner with Ray Curran, a man who excelled in business and life. It was a sultry summer evening and we sat on the veranda overlooking the elegant River Thames at Sonning. It was one of those catch-up kind of chats.

Before long, my thoughts took me faster and faster towards even more confusion. All the while, Ray listened patiently. He never intervened and waited until I'd run out of steam. I had been giving all the reasons why I couldn't go home to Ireland. The more I talked, the more I reinforced that dreadful thought.

Then, when I'd finished, Ray looked me in the eye and said: "That, Conor, is 'sequential thinking'. Just go home. Those obstacles are in your mind. They are not real. Go home, just do it".

They were simple words but they were powerful words. Behind the simplicity lay a deep lesson that I've never lost. You just do it and you never let obstacles become your personal prison. You can do anything you want.

Lord Ballyedmond

By coincidence, I was in the company of Eddie Haughey, founder of Norbrook Laboratories and better known as Lord Ballyedmond (who sadly died in a helicopter crash as I was finalising this book). I was sitting opposite him at dinner. He told me the story of how he founded Norbrook Laboratories and how his vision set him apart from many others. However, it was his self-belief that I remembered most. True self-belief isn't remotely related to arrogance or confidence. It is simply that, self-belief.

Towards the end of our conversation, I had just one question I wanted to ask. It was this: "If you hadn't founded Norbrook, what would you have done?".

His reply, quick as a flash, was instant and instinctive: "Anything I wanted to, Conor, anything I wanted to".

So can I, so can you.

CHAPTER 3
IMPORTANT QUESTIONS FOR YOU

I was dyslexic, I had no understanding of schoolwork whatsoever. I certainly would have failed IQ tests. And it was one of the reasons I left school when I was 15 years old. And if I'm not interested in something, I don't grasp it.
Richard Branson

Can I sell? Of course, you can.

Do I want to? That's a different question – but let's find out.

The greatest driver of success is the desire to do what inspires you and what you believe in. Passion, honesty and attitude will overcome a multitude of weaknesses and no amount of skill will compensate if the underlying truth is money, greed or exploitation. We are bound by our limitations and there's not much point in pursuing an intriguing career if the fundamentals are missing.

These fundamentals fall into two categories. The first is all about emotions, values and attitude; the second is grounding those assets in skill, ability and technique.

Combine the two and success will follow. Equally, if one side is missing, you will be a little like the rowing boat with oarsmen on one side only.

The First Nine – All about Passion

Read the statements below and write either *Yes* or a *No* beside each one:

- I really love the work I do.
- I'm never ever bored.
- I am passionate about learning more.
- I spend free time learning.

- I'm very happy when I'm working independently.
- I do what I do because I want to make a difference.
- I like to have control over my future as well as my income.
- I like the idea of the harder I work, the more I succeed or earn.
- I love being creative when solving problems.

Did you write *Yes* against each question? That's the goal.

Really successful sales people combine the approach, attitude and characteristics of the nine questions above. They want to control their destiny, be independent and enjoy the daily challenges of problem-solving, learning and being busy.

The Next Eight Questions – All about Faith

Again, write *Yes* or *No* against each statement:

- I believe that sales and selling are the responsibility of everyone in my organisation.
- I believe that everyone in our company influences customers in some way.
- I really do understand not just my company but also my industry.
- My industry excites and intrigues me.
- I have absolute faith in what we do and what we sell.
- I believe that our customers truly benefit from buying from us.
- I get frustrated if they don't see how much this will help them.
- I am absolutely confident in our company, product, service and future.

Again, you should be answering *Yes* to all eight questions.

This section is about belief. In simple terms, it's about knowing how good you are and how this will benefit your customer. What's the objective? It is still to make your customers' lives better, easier and more productive.

And these eight questions link back to the first nine since, if you don't have true passion, I simply won't believe you.

The Next 10 Questions – All about Knowledge

Again, write *Yes* or *No* against each statement:

- I know how my product will benefit my customer.
- I know what makes us truly different.
- I know how our product will give our customer competitive advantage.
- I know our message.
- I know how to express it.
- I know the objections and how to answer them.
- I am absolutely clear about whom I need to speak to.
- I know what I will tell them to make them want to see me.
- I really understand the customer's priorities and motivations.
- I have researched the customer's company in detail.

There is nothing worse than the inexperienced sales person who wings it. They may get away with it once but it won't last. Nothing breaks trust more rapidly.

The Final Six – All about Emotions

Again, write *Yes* or *No* against each statement:

- I do what is right for my customer regardless of its impact on me.
- I would give him a huge free sample because I know he will see how good it is.
- I say "No" if it is not the right thing for my customer.
- I'm patient even if I'm in a hurry.
- I understand the pressures he is under in making the right decision.
- I will never break the trust he has shown in me.

How Did You Do?

Review all of the 33 statements. For each *Yes*, give yourself 3 points. For each *No*, give yourself no points. Now add up your points:

- If you scored **80** or more, you are a sales superstar;
- If you scored **60** or more, you are good but a little more learning and experience will help;
- If you scored **40** or more, you might begin to ask yourself whether you are on the right path;
- If you scored **20** or more, you may just have ended up in that unplanned cul-de-sac.

CHAPTER 4
I'M IN SALES –
OR IS IT MARKETING?

If I look confused, it is because I am thinking.
Samuel Goldwyn

What's the difference between Sales and Marketing?

Lots of people confuse sales with marketing. It's understandable because the route to sales is often a detour in what was really meant to be a marketing career. I know, I was there.

My very first job with a slow-moving State company quickly labelled me as a 'Marketing Management Trainee'. Translated, it meant they had no idea what to do with me. An easy solution was to bury me under this wonderfully ambiguous title that meant I could be deployed to do anything.

Marketing and Sales are entirely different skills: two halves of a whole – but independent. There are so many academic definitions that even the most passionate learner can be forgiven for confusing the two. Why is it that some books take the simple and make it complex?

The purpose of marketing is simply to create the desire to buy – nothing else. The purpose of selling is to ensure the desire to buy converts into a commercial transaction. They are separate journeys, requiring different skills.

Of course, the lines between marketing and sales can overlap and blur a little. Is what I am doing 'Marketing' or 'Sales'?

The answer comes when you ask yourself whether you are still creating the desire to buy. Marketing, put simply, is everything you do to gain attention – and, from there, the desire to buy.

PR, social media, press coverage, websites, advertising, awards and more are all tools used in marketing to create the desire to buy. They are fundamentally messages and signals. Their purpose is to attract you, to make you take notice and to make you want what it is they are offering.

This 'want' must come first. The sale follows.

Imagine a bleak winter day. The sky is dull grey and the landscape is a little barren. Your mood, which is always an emotional decision-maker, matches the weather.

On a long frosty, dreary drive, you round a bend to see a sun-drenched poster of perfect people on a perfect beach. Their smiles, tans and sense of fun stir your senses. You want to be there.

Of course, you can't stop at the massive billboard and reach out to feel the sun or the sand. You can't buy and you can't even make an enquiry. But, it has planted the seed and created the desire to buy. It's not a coincidence that you went online that night to pick out your next holiday. You probably didn't even analyse why.

The meeting, the phone call, or the online sales form completes the process. They've made a sale and you just bought. You have given money for what you are about to receive.

Why did you buy? Because the marketing process created the desire. Without it, it is unlikely that you'd have thought about a holiday at that moment on that drive.

Which One Am I?

According to John Jantsch, the difference between marketing and sales is that Marketing owns the message and Sales owns the relationship. This is a perfect summary of the difference.

Marketing is all about the message and how to create it; sales is all about the relationship and how to evolve it. One involves excellence with communication; the other excellence with people.

Only you can decide which fits you. Rarely is one person the master of both.

Titles

Every day, I meet Sales & Marketing Directors. The title always intrigues me – because it's the wrong way around. It should be Marketing & Sales Director.

Marketing always comes first; sales follow.

In some ways, the art of selling is a much more complex challenge. After all, you are dealing with people, emotions, agendas and different motivations.

Great sales people are really good at reading people and have an enormous desire to problem-solve and to help their customers.

Are you the master of messages or the master of relationships? Your instinctive answer will guide you to the correct fit.

CHAPTER 5
IS THIS REALLY ME?

George Foreman. A miracle. A mystery to myself. Who am I? The mirror says back, "The George you was always meant to be". Wasn't always like that. Used to look in the mirror and cried a river.
George Foreman

If you ask 10 sales people what motivates them, you will probably get 10 different answers. Some will say *"to make money"*, others will say *"to create customers"*, and most will say *"to reach my target"*. Of course, none of these are intrinsically wrong but they are more a consequence than a motive.

Sales people are a tarnished lot. The abiding images of the dodgy used car salesman or the salesman who tricked you into buying sub-standard double glazing are hard to erase. Television has made them into enduring comic characters and those labels can be hard to lose.

There are three primary reasons why really good sales people are really good sales people:

- The first is simply that they love what they do;
- The second is an enormous desire to serve and to make their customers' lives easier;
- The third is that they work very hard.

But the money that flows into their overflowing pockets is never the goal, it is simply the consequence of all three attributes.

I Don't Like Mondays

If you don't like Mondays, then you don't like your job. If you don't like your job, you can't be good at it. If you agree with the above, you are probably in the wrong job. Tough but true – but don't despair. Sometimes, you have to clean out the familiar cupboard to make way for something new and something better.

When I was in college, *The Boomtown Rats* were just about the biggest and coolest band going. Bob Geldof, now Sir Bob, was a rebellious Pied Piper who said what we only thought. We loved it. Their songs have become classics and, like all good lessons, their lyrics are timeless, sharp and evocative.

I Don't Like Mondays always stood out. It paints a picture of dread that we have all experienced at some point. Equally, we have tasted the euphoria of Fridays and, if you have been there too, you are probably in the wrong job.

To succeed in selling – in fact, to succeed at anything – the motivation must never be 'a job'. It must be the realisation of a passion. If your work reflects who you are you will succeed; if it doesn't, you won't. A career that excites you, inspires you and engages you will allow you to never see any difference between Monday and Friday.

I know, I once was where you might be now.

The Right Job – Selling Desks

We can easily end up stuck in the cul-de-sac of a job we really hate. It's soul-destroying. It can seep into every aspect of life and numb your senses. It is a dreadful way to live.

Like most people, I took a wrong turn into an apparently attractive dead-end. I was selling desks. Nothing can be more tedious, dreary and dull. Of course, I was looking at the products, not the customer. That was half the problem but I just couldn't get excited by desks. It didn't take a prospective customer long to spot my all-consuming lack of enthusiasm. The spiral down was deadly, slow and inevitable. Sooner or later, there was going to be a loud crash. It came.

She was cheerful, blonde and buxom. She laughed, she sang and was happy. We worked for the same company. She adored her job, I hated mine. I couldn't understand the difference.

In the canteen, we met over coffee. It was unplanned. Clearly, I was a gloomy cloud interrupting her sunshine.

"Cheer up, Conor, this is probably as good as it gets for you in your career".

I must have appeared haunted and dangerous because she hotfooted it out of the room.

It was a defining moment and a moment that made me realise I was in the wrong industry and job. It was also a choice: stay and suck it up or go and do something about it.

I did something about it – more on that later.

To succeed in selling, you must love your industry, colleagues, company and job. Most of all, you have to love your customers. If you don't, you won't succeed and life will be a series of unnecessary highs and lows.

Passion or Pleasure?

Being great at anything is as much about attitude as it is about the art and the science or even the skill.

Being really good with customers comes from loving your customers. If you don't love your customers, you can't love your job. Great service is really just about a great attitude, which can only be born out of passion.

We live in a brand-driven culture, yet we forget to ask ourselves, *"What is my brand?"*. What is it you stand for? What are your values? What drives you, inspires you and excites you? What do you like doing and what do you not like doing?

It's easy to answer these questions about ourselves.

It's not so easy to make sure they match our career.

Success comes when we do. Failure is inevitable when we don't. If you like what you do, there's no such thing as hard work. Yes, there will be complex work, challenging work and even difficult work – but no 'hard' work.

For a company, there isn't anything worse than the brand promising me all good things and the delivery being quite the opposite.

The salesperson becomes our understanding of the brand. Watch how people often say, "I can't stand X Company. Their service, attitude and approach is appalling". Of course, what they really mean is that their encounter with one particular person in that company was all of the above.

"Try Harder"

The flight to the UK was late. An important presentation loomed and the stress was building. We were up against a very important clock.

My business companion that day was a 'wise owl' with a track record of developing successful brands. He was – always is – calm, mannerly and never irrational.

Late, we got to the desk of the big car rental company. Our urgency and near panic was clear for all to see, with the exception of our road-blocking, obstructive customer service agent, whose name badge told us her name was Sarah.

"We are really in a rush and we would like to pick up our car as soon as possible, please, Sarah."

Glancing at her finely-honed nails indifferently, she said, "I'm sorry, sir, I've no record of your booking".

My calm companion was unbowed. "Try harder, Sarah", he said.

Suppressing a cynical yawn, she retorted instantly with "I am doing my best, sir".

His demeanour didn't change. Again, he said, "Try harder, Sarah".

It went on like this for several minutes. Even I was beginning to wonder about the "Try harder" refrain.

Eventually, we got our car and we were on our way – late.

He wasn't finished yet. Before he turned away from her desk, he smiled, looked at her directly and said, "Oh, by the way, Sarah, very nice badge".

I was as perplexed as Sarah.

She looked down at her badge. What did it say?

"We try harder."

You see, a brand cannot be independent of its people. If it is, there is no brand. If you don't want to try harder, you're in the wrong job and it's not the customer's fault no matter how interesting your finely-honed nails. It will always come back to that simple line: *"If you don't love your customers, you can't love your job"*.

Nurses

A few years ago, I found myself humming along to that very cheesy song, *Everybody's Free (To Wear Sunscreen)*, by Baz Luhrmann.

One day, early for an appointment, I had time on my hands. This time, I listened – usually, I just heard. Very quickly, I forgot the tune; I was hypnotised by the words. The 'cheesy' song was no longer cheesy: it was smart, bright, deep and useful.

One line in particular stood out. It said: *"The real troubles in your life are apt to be things that never crossed your worried mind; the kind that blindside you at 4pm on some idle Tuesday"*.

It startled me. It was a simple and defining moment. *"So true"*, I thought. All the horrible (and fantastic) events in my life were never, ever, the things I thought I saw coming.

But, when you come to terms with whatever event unseated you, there are so many new and wonderful learnings that come your way. Inevitably, growth lies on the far side of something challenging or difficult.

My '4pm Tuesday moment' came out of the blue. It wasn't remotely on my radar. I had inherited a silent genetic condition. Discovered in time, as it was, it is absolutely non-threatening in any way. However, it meant that, after a life of dodging doctors, nurses and especially needles, I was going to have to get used to all three – and every week until they righted my listing ship.

Of course, this is not intended as a depressing tale of woe, or even about me, it is a tale of discovery and discovering the difference between a job and a vocation.

❖

On a very wet, windy and dark winter morning, I arrived at the hospital ridiculously early. My appointment was for 8.15am; I was there at 7:30am. Taking a deep breath, I crossed the threshold.

In recession, our creaking and overburdened care system fell apart. Everything was cut. As always, it's the front line that is asked to bear the brunt. I was early but Ann-Marie gave me a welcome that the best five-star hotel would be proud of. More importantly, her calm, gentle manner washed away my fear. Reassuring, kind and patient, you just couldn't be in better hands.

Over time, I got to know her colleagues, Caroline and Deirdre. They share the same values – care, compassion and concern. In an era when Government is cutting costs in every sector, it would be understandable for front line workers to do only what they are paid to do with their ever-reducing pay for ever-increasing hours. Nobody could argue with that.

My appointment was scheduled every week for 8:15am, the first appointment of the day. In conversation, I told Ann-Marie that it was usually close to 8am when I arrived. Her reply said it all: "If you're here early, come in. We don't start until 8:15am but I'm in for 7:30 anyway. Come in and we will look after you".

They sure did.

I learned, at first hand, that those who are what they do never get caught up in politics, gossip or moaning. They are too busy delivering the things that really matter. That's why they are so good at what they do. It is who they are. It's not their job, it's their vocation and their purpose.

A Beautiful Letter

Edenderry, in County Offaly, still retains much of its rural market town feel although motorways and technology have done their best to make it conform to the fast-paced, modern life that we call the 'norm'. Thankfully, it has resisted.

In the heart of the town lies Patrick Larkin's Pub. Three generations have successfully run it, through three different eras. Today, Patrick Senior is handing the reins to Patrick Junior, just like his father before him.

Some years ago, I received a letter from Patrick Senior. It stood out for two reasons. First, it said *"Thank you"* for the work we had done together. In itself, that was rare. But, second, in the body of his beautifully inked letter, he talked about his customers. His line is forever etched in my memory: *"I have had the privilege to live with the people of Edenderry and I have been proud to serve them".*

It was the word 'privilege' that stood out and then the 'proud to serve' phrase. It made me think about myself and the many people in sales that I've met. How many would use these terms? How many wanted to serve? It is no surprise that the Larkins' business has endured when many have fallen.

CHAPTER 6
IN SEARCH OF SALES

Be a yardstick of quality. Some people aren't used to an environment where excellence is expected.
Steve Jobs

The Tiny Picture in a Tiny Window

I was living in London and as poor as a church mouse. The West End was an intriguing place and it was always fun to watch the aristocracy go shopping. Chauffeurs tipped their caps at elderly ladies stooped under the weight of priceless gold and sparkly heirlooms. Gentlemen were gentlemen and country tweeds cut a dash in the City. Smart shops competed on every corner. Tradition married quality and the customers came. Every square inch was stuffed with messages and merchandise. It was a little overpowering even to the poor window-shopping apprentice. Still, it smelt of money, class and elegance.

Alfred Dunhill is a beautiful brand. In many ways, the ultimate gentleman's brand and, as a young man, I dreamed of buying even their smallest goods. I took in the beautiful products outside and wondered if I'd ever own such fine things.

One small empty window caught my eye. Unlike all the other windows, this one was empty. I peered in, a little confused.

It wasn't as empty as I had thought. Sitting, all alone, in the window was a tiny silver picture frame. It was so small you almost had to strain to see it. I strained and it drew me in closer.

The marvellous italic inky script scratched out a message I never forgot: *"Quality is remembered long after price is forgotten"*.

A Nasty Picture

Dan Norton ran a very successful business in the heart of Dublin. Dan was a small man with a huge warm personality. He had charisma and kindness. He started out selling typewriters to the nuns and soon they fell in love with him too. For years, we had flirted with the idea of my working with him. Inevitably, I did.

Dan enjoyed beautiful things. His immaculate tailor-made suits cut a dash on the dreariest day. His Mercedes Benz looked huge and his warmth lit up every occasion. But it was his office that used to intrigue me most. It was mahogany-panelled, with a wonderful handmade polished desk inlaid with a rich green leather top. His chair looked like a throne and his desk was always clear. However, I was always surprised by the lack of anything on the walls of his office: no pictures, no paintings, nothing. It made a beautiful room a little soulless. It confused me.

One day, he asked me to pop in to his office. When I got there, I instantly spotted a picture hanging on the previously barren wall. It was a print, in a cheap frame, of a man on a camel high in the desert overlooking endless sand dunes. The man was using his hand to shield his view from the overpowering sun. It was a lonely and slightly sad image. It clashed with everything else.

"What do you think of my new picture, Conor?", Dan asked.

Not wanting to upset or offend him, I went for safety. "It's nice", I replied unconvincingly.

What Dan said next was one of those simple lessons that I have never lost. I hope you will remember it too.

"It's not a nice picture, Conor. It's quite a horrible picture actually. But, it tells a very important story for all of us who have to sell".

I listened intently, not knowing where this story could possibly go.

Dan continued: "You see, the man high on the camel, high up in the dunes, is just like you and me. He is in a barren place. He has some food, some clothing and a camel that's getting tired. He's a little lost. Conor, he is just like the salesman. He has had a little luck but needs to keep going to avoid failure. He is you and me. What do you think he is doing right now? He is looking far into the distance wondering where his next sale is coming from. Isn't that what you and I have to do every day?".

Before you mount your camel, be sure it's a journey you want to take.

The One Thing

When he walked into the training room, he sighed. His heavy frame caused a dull thump as he fell into his seat. He owned the business.

I started the workshop conscious of his intense disinterest. His eyes stayed parallel to the table top and his intermittent loud deep breath distracted everyone. His loyal staff had seen it all before.

We were talking, training and teaching 'sales'. My audience were young and eager. The owner was neither. I kept to my mission despite it all.

Slowly, we worked our way through the morning and made good progress. For my sighing friend, it was not quick enough. The sighs found a new friend in his right hand. A pencil. The sighs were joined by the slow tap tap of the pencil on the hard plastic table. Tap pause tap pause tap pause tap. It was hard to focus but I was determined to teach the eager managers. Each tap was another tiny bit burnt off the ever-decreasing fuse. It wouldn't be long before he exploded.

With arms stretching wide and a chest puffed out behind a shirt whose buttons were tested to the limits, he finally burst: "Yes, yes, this is all very fine but …".

We waited for his incisive view. It came quickly.

"I've listened to this and I've listened to that but, what I want to know is: What is the one thing you are going to say or do that's going to transform our sales performance?"

He poured enormous emphasis on the words *"one thing"*. He wanted the Holy Grail, nothing less would do.

I let him finish. I took my time. I wanted everything to settle so he would really listen to my answer. The room went quiet.

"Nothing", I said.

He looked angry and quickly replied, *"Nothing?"*.

"That's right", I said. "Nothing. Sales and selling is a combination of technique, attitude, character, values, skill and passion, with many other ingredients thrown in. There is no easy answer. It's a complex business and, if I were you, I'd beware any man who tells you it's just 'one thing'".

With a spectacular sigh, he stood up and walked out.

It's funny but his business followed suit four years later.

Naturally Gifted

As a young salesman immersed in the excitement of London, I always believed I would gain riches based on natural talent. I even thought I could think my way to the top. I held the belief so strongly that I scoffed at my colleague Alan.

Alan was a really nice guy but, when we went out to play, Alan stayed behind. We thought he was a nice guy, but not much fun. Alan kept working.

Every year, Alan earned about twice as much as the rest of us. Secretly, we envied him but having fun was too important in the scheme of things. That was a price we couldn't pay. Alan did.

Of course, Alan knew what had not yet dawned on us. Success was nothing to do with natural talent and everything to do with hard work. Oh, and attitude too.

One day, we were all plotting an early escape to some local hostelry. Just before we left for the pub, I popped over to Alan and asked him if he was joining us. In his cheerful, charming way, he said a definite "No". Deep down, I admired his resolve.

As I left for yet more fun and far less work, I heard his conversation with a customer. It went something like this.

"Of course I can be with you at 6am. It really isn't a problem, and I love getting into the City early".

Whether he did or not wasn't important. He was prepared to do what his customer wanted. More importantly, he took away the barriers and he even persuaded them that he enjoyed 4am starts from his home.

Alan went on to be very successful and very wealthy – no surprise.

To be great in sales and selling, you can't 'think' your way to the top. It takes dedication, persistence and doing everything your inner soul tells you not to do. That's the common denominator in great sales people. They see the goal, not the journey.

CHAPTER 7
UNDERSTANDING THE IMPACT WE MAKE

Anger and intolerance are the enemies of correct understanding.
Mahatma Gandhi

Great sales and great selling are simple. It's often the human condition that throws the spanner into the melting pot.

To succeed in selling – to really succeed – you must have a potent mix of character (who you are) and skill (what you can do). In other words, you need both the art and the science.

Then, there is your attitude to customers. Some people clearly consider the customer as the opposition, others as their reason to exist. Each group is rooted in their own values, ego, conflicts and past.

Some years ago, I asked a group of people to define great service. I got lots of 'exceeding customers' expectations' and sound bites you've heard before. One definition stood out and is memorable: *"Good service is love in work clothes"*. That captures everything.

How we see ourselves, how we see others and how happy we are will manifest itself very quickly. If you don't like your job, you can't succeed. If you do, you will.

Bad Cop

I was heading home from the sun. The mood was calm and everything was on time. There was no stress. Everyone boarded politely and I was lucky enough to sit in the front row. I was people-watching because that's what people in sales do.

He was happy, she was sad. He was grumpy, she was patient. Every mood made its way on board. It was just another day, just another flight.

The Chief Stewardess had a different view. It wasn't our flight. Oh no, it was *her* flight. I watched amused. It was as if she was hoping for trouble. Like a restless boxer, she seemed to bounce up and down provoking the unprovoked with a look, a nudge or a defiant, dismissive gesture. Oh yes, it sure was her flight.

We took off. The flight was relaxed and people basked in their post-holiday peacefulness. Everyone melted back into their own world. I had one eye closed and the other keeping a wary eye on the Chief. She seemed disappointed. There was no battle to fight, no trouble and no loud passengers. That was about to change.

A young and cheerful chap committed the mortal sin of drinking some liquor from his illegal stash. It was time to pounce.

Tannoy ready, arms folded, deep breath. She said, with utter disdain in her voice: "Anyone drinking their own alcohol on board this flight can expect to be arrested on arrival".

Now, both my eyes were wide open – as was my jaw. The passengers froze in a stiff silence. I was intrigued more than astonished. Why would someone attack a sleeping village?

I decided to engage the Chief as she sat opposite. I asked her whether they got much trouble on this particular route.

"Oh God, no, this one is mild. It's the flight from X that really gets the dregs of society".

Clearly, the Chief was not a fan of customers.

I said no more for fear of instant extradition, deportation or execution. She smiled the contented smile of one who over had just over-indulged at the sumptuous feast.

Good Cop

In 1995, we were coming home to Ireland from Boston. Two ordinary young people on a tight budget and grateful for a family holiday. Patiently, we joined the check-in line and everything was normal until it was our turn.

The smiling check-in man took our passports and asked us to bear with him. We were anxious, nervous even. What had we done? This was unusual.

He was back in no time. Again, his broad smile was warming and put us at ease.

"We would like to upgrade you to First Class", he said cheerily.

Our reply was, "We think you've made a mistake. Have you mixed us up with someone else?".

He hadn't.

We went upstairs sheepishly and almost apologised to be intruding on the great and the good. The size of the seats made us laugh, and we wondered were they clocking up a secret bill for the drinks they pushed into our hand.

What stood out most? It wasn't the luxury, indulgence or even opulence, it was very simply that we were treated to the same five-star service as the very famous actor sitting across from us.

The bad cop story was just six months ago. The good cop, 18 years ago.

In 18 more years, I expect the bad cop story will still have wings. Aren't you reading it now?

The Smiling Invisible Man

Some time ago, I wrote a short paragraph as I waited in the very polished corporate reception area of a large and prestigious organisation.

I was early and I had time to kill. I watched people come and go: their moods, their attitude and their response. Some people doodle, some dream, I write.

This is what I wrote:

Have you seen me?

I'm that regular customer who is often in your place. I'm a little shy, just normal and very patient. I'm so patient that I watch with a slight soft smile as your staff dash here, dash there, but never seem to notice me.

Sometimes, I look on and watch your staff enjoying a little gossip. I smile then too. They don't realise that I can hear them, and I'm amazed they don't even see me. It's funny though, because sometimes they are gossiping about their company, their boss, their job and even about those 'nasty little creatures' we call customers. Yet, they never see me standing right under their nose and listening to their every word.

As the invisible man, I see everything but those beautifully-dressed professionals seem to see nothing.

Often, I will go into a beautiful comfy and cosy reception area. I will admire the expensive furniture, the features and the beautiful paintings, but I will wonder too. I'll wonder if the smart receptionist with the smart uniform is alive ... or maybe just another feature? I'll marvel at the speed they chew gum. I'll wonder why they are fixated by their nails, PC or phone, and I'll be amazed at how they never even notice my entrance or my presence!

To many, I'm just that ordinary guy we call the guest, the client or the customer. But, to my friends, family and colleagues, I'm a little more than that, I might even be a little bit special.

You see, I'm that regular average guy who everyday makes the wheels of industry turn. There are lots of me – in fact, thousands and millions. I represent the majority, not the few, and I represent the invisible customer everywhere.

But I'm smiling my wry smile again. Any idea why? Thing is, I'm not stupid. Though invisible to you, I do see everything. I also see choice, options and alternatives ... and ... I know my 'rights'. I have just exercised those 'rights' and guess what? …. I won't be back, no matter what.

Why am I still smiling my wry smile? Well, it tickles me that every day and every year your company spends so much money advertising for me to come to you. Funny thing is, if you had opened your eyes in the first place, I was already there!

But now, I'm gone.

It's one thing for those clever chaps in marketing to create an ideal company full of ideal people and even idealism. The world is not like that.

Of course, the simple point is that age-old maxim: *"Under-promise and over-deliver"*. If you can't do that, don't promise it. If you do, you'll let me down and that's just as bad as letting your own brand down.

"Trust Me"

Trust is fundamental to any relationship. Without trust, you won't have sales. If I don't trust you, I won't buy from you. Simple, unfailing and final.

Trust is the timeless bedrock of every successful career and sales career. It is the glue in every relationship.

Trust is earned, not promised. Trust is at the very core of every encounter and every relationship.

One Sunday, in London, I indulged in that very British habit of coffee and *The Sunday Times* in a little café just off the King's Road. I can't remember the content, thesis or story but I do remember the first line of one article I read that Sunday. In fact, it has stayed with me for a very long time and never failed to act as an excellent compass. What did that first line say?

"Beware the man who says 'Trust me'."

You can't bestow trust. You can't dispense it. In fact, you don't even control it. The other person does.

It would be easy to spend our lives in a constant state of mistrust that, in itself, would probably be a worse fate. Sometimes, to reach somewhere new, you have to take risks and probe boundaries. That is what every pioneer does.

Business is no different. In the early stages of a relationship, we seek out trust signals and we process them quickly and usually by instinct. "The best way to find out if you can trust somebody is to trust them", as Ernest Hemingway said.

Recently, I sat in on a workshop given by a wise colleague. Like every learning situation, we take away some little pieces that have an impact way beyond their size. This time, it was a quote from American author Mark Twain that has echoed long into everything we do: *"If you tell the truth, you don't have to remember anything"*.

Now, rewind your learning head and think back to the leaders who weren't leaders, the pirates who got some power and, worst of all, the man who said, *"Trust me"*.

Somehow, I'll bet you didn't.

Online Reviews

I love this piece of wisdom that reflects our online age: *"Everyone has become a reporter"*. It is so easy to have a voice *via* self-publishing and for your words to travel fast – for good or for evil or even for self-gain.

That quote also reminded me of the little calendar I once saw with those quirky daily quotes. Whilst many of them were a little cheesy, one stood out. It said: *"There are many things I have regretted saying but I never regretted saying nothing"*.

It's a line that has saved me many times when emotion would have overruled common-sense. Before you write anything online, you should ask yourself would you be happy for your words to appear in the papers, or maybe even in the Law Courts?

It was a new business and she needed a head-start. Of course, a good business evolves very slowly and culture follows. But quite quickly, the online reviews were stunning. Almost daily, they trickled in, giving rave reviews. No flaws, just perfection. Any honest reader would have thought they'd discovered Heaven. For those less innocent, it created suspicion, especially when so many work so hard to receive applause half as frequently.

"Did you see all the fantastic reviews online?", said my friend Peter. A rather astute man, a policeman, he then asked, "What did you think of them?".

"Well, they certainly seem fantastic" came my guarded response.

"Of course, they're fantastic", said he. "She writes them herself".

Naturally, curiosity got the upper hand. You see, my grandfather was a Guard and my mother would have been an even better detective. I've inherited the gene.

"How do you know?", I asked.

He smiled and, quick as you like, said, "She spells the same word wrong in every review".

"Look At His Shoes"

Sometimes, maybe even often, it is the smallest thing that creates the biggest impact.

I, and a few colleagues, were invited to meet a man. He was well-known and successful in his chosen industry. We met, we talked and we retreated to think.

My instincts were flashing warning lights, an uneasy feeling filled my senses. Not something I could put my finger on but just uneasy.

I said little. I wanted to hear what my colleagues had to say. The words were right, the contract too, we just couldn't find ourselves saying *Yes.*

Experience teaches you to listen to instincts. You mightn't always understand them but you don't have to. The mistake is to ignore them. We bashed it about but still we couldn't resolve our instincts with our desire to do a good job.

The tipping point arrived in a very unusual way.

"Did you see his shoes?", said my learned friend.

"No", said I.

"Have a look at them later", said he.

I did – game over.

"Cheap, broken and unpolished" came the observations of my comrades.

They didn't need to explain. In one sentence, the scales had tipped. If he didn't care about his shoes, he didn't care. At least, that's what we concluded. Time would prove us right.

You can't represent a good brand if your own presentation is different, especially if you are the owner.

The Man's Shop

I had heard about this little man's shop. I'd seen its smart exterior and the messages promised tradition, excellence and trust. I was halfway to buying already. I was looking forward to a dashing new suit. It wasn't long before 'dashing' became dashed.

I waited patiently as the tailor tended a customer. The customer was clearly well-to-do and his short rotund frame betrayed a fondness for life's treats. Obviously successful, he was placing his image in the tailor's hands. Listening to the dialogue, it mattered to him very much.

In the meantime, I was admiring the beautiful suits and, even though the price tags made me wince, I stayed on, inviting myself into his sale.

The small cheerful gentleman donned the jacket of his suit and went energetically to the full-length mirror. His bubble deflated a little at the sight before him. In a slightly querulous tone, he said, "Are you sure, really sure, this looks good on me?".

The tailor didn't flinch. "It looks superb on you. Amazing. Perfect". The superlatives continued and with only a tiny bit of resistance, the purchase was made.

The trousers were too long and didn't fit. The shoulders of the jacket were built for someone with a wingspan of at least another foot. The sleeves shrouded his knuckles and the jacket over hung his knees. With *"perfect fit"* ringing in my ears, I left.

Within the year, the shop had closed.

More Boomtown Rats

My very first job, fresh from college, was with our then State design company, Kilkenny Design Workshops. It was a wonderful start because the environment was pioneering, creative and always pursuing excellence. As part of my training and induction, I became a shop assistant for six months, selling very high-end domestic furniture.

Saturday was hectic, but the rest of the week could be tedious. That didn't sit well, I don't like doing nothing.

It was an idle Monday and the store was especially quiet. You could hear a pin drop.

He was a small guy. A little scruffy in well-worn denims. He was unshaven and maybe even a little tired-looking after the weekend. He didn't say much. He just rambled around looking at everything. With little else to do, I watched him like a hawk. In my mind, he couldn't afford our very expensive goods nor did he fit our 'typical' customer. I was suspicious. I began to follow him discreetly and eventually pounced.

"Can I help you?", I enquired, probably betraying a slight aloof cynicism.

"Yes, please", he replied politely. "How much is this? How much are three of those and two of these?"

Looking disinterested and probably in a hasty desire to end this uncomfortable charade, I gave him the price.

"Ok, I'll take two sofas, four of those wardrobes, three of these chests of drawers, two dining tables, eight dining chairs …" and on it went.

In my head, I went, *"Yeah right! I'll call his bluff"*.

"Certainly, sir, let's go to the cashpoint."

Without blinking, he said, "Sure".

The bill was huge. So huge it must have been a record for the biggest single sale in the store's history. I gave him the total and considered calling security.

For the second time, he didn't blink. He produced his chequebook and my mouth dropped. Printed on the tatty cheque book was his name: 'Pete Briquette'.

Now *my* jaw hit the floor.

Pete Briquette (*aka* Peter Cusack) was the bass guitarist for *The Boomtown Rats*, probably one of the world's biggest bands then.

He bought. It was a retail record and I've never rushed to judge a customer since then. Besides teaching me never to rush to judgement, it taught me that really high achievers are humble. Then again, isn't that why they are achievers?

The Very Tight T-shirt

Reading your customers is half the battle to building rapport, the bedrock of good relationships. Get it right and you'll succeed in selling more.

Above all, rapport must be honest, humble and real. That means observing, listening and reading the clues.

Mick Dowling is a boxer and an Olympian – not once but twice. He is also a European Bronze medallist. His good wife, Emily, won the Dublin Marathon and represented Ireland for nine years in cross-country international competition. In recent years, Emily won a World Masters silver medal.

Sitting on a sofa in their house one day, I felt an cold hard object poking uncomfortably into my right thigh. I plunged my hand deep into the sofa's innards to wrestle out this annoyance. In my hand, I held Emily's World Masters silver medal. Emily's response said all there is to say about humility and knowing what matters in life: "Is that where it is? Isn't that funny. I've been looking for it for ages".

More than anything, Mick and Emily have been very good friends for many years. One evening, we went out to dinner. Conversation, stories and laughter flowed. It was the norm on such evenings.

This particular evening, the weather was warm. The *maître d'*, whom I knew, introduced himself. He knew me, but not Mick and Emily. He is a very pleasant chap but tends to stay just a little too long and his favourite subject is himself. This time, he was setting a record. We wondered when he might leave.

What really caught our eye was the figure-hugging spray-on pure white t-shirt he wore. It was sparkling, out of place and showed a torso that was only three-quarters of the way to being toned. As Emily might say when coaching our running, "Not bad, but more to do".

When conversation ground to a halt, I foolishly asked him if he was working out. I lit a fuse that burnt far longer than we expected. He launched into a monologue about his regime, diet and discipline. Mick and Emily showed tremendous empathy and support for his Herculean efforts. They even smiled approvingly.

As he spoke, he even managed to unwittingly flex his biceps a little. This time, we all smiled.

Eventually, he came up for breath and, by now, we knew every moment of his rigorous fitness routine. He paused, looked Mick in the eye and said: "You look quite fit yourself, Mick. Do you work out yourself?" .

Mick, as fast as his right-hand upper cut, replied, "Ah, just a bit, now and then".

Our *maître d'*, not picking up the hint, immediately responded: "Good man, keep up the good work. At this stage of our lives, we are hardly going to the Olympics".

Mick smiled and said knowingly, "I guess not".

CHAPTER 8
UNDERSTANDING EMOTIONS AND PEOPLE

When dealing with people, remember you are not dealing with creatures of logic, but creatures of emotion.
Dale Carnegie

We are disappointed when a machine breaks. It might have been unfailingly reliable for 20 years but we get cross and might even give it a little kick.

"Why, oh why are you doing this to me?"

The machine doesn't reply. It gets another kick. We are being silly, even if we feel morally superior to the poor overworked machine.

Of course, it is our emotions that differentiate us from everything else. They're complex little things, emotions, and, over time, they learn bad habits and gather toxic moss. On the other hand, the purity of a child having fun is because they have not yet 'learnt' all the negative emotions like fear, doubt, insecurity and more.

Like it or not, emotions play an enormous part in buying and in selling. Often, we are not practical, rational beings. At its simplest, *"I just don't like him"* is enough to cause a potential buyer to walk away, even at their own expense. People will rarely buy from people they don't like and will only do so when there's no alternative. People, where possible, will buy from friends.

However, the opposite in sales of 'not being liked' is not 'to be liked', it is to be respected. There's a difference.

As a former student of philosophy and psychology, I have a deep interest in how we motivate people and what it is we do to inhibit our own growth and the growth of others. Philosophy is often described as the study of wisdom. For me, it's simpler, it is all about 'Why?' and the desire to understand.

To succeed in selling, you must understand emotions, sense them and know how to manage them. Most times, we won't have any idea they exist in a customer and, if you do, you certainly won't know where they're coming from. And, unless you're a psychologist or psychotherapist, you don't need to. Your job is to understand emotions, not treat them. Great sales people manage two sets of emotions: their own and their customer's.

Emotions

Emotions lie beneath; behaviour is what we see. Emotions can manifest themselves in many ways: fear, anxiety, disinterest, distrust, cynicism, sarcasm, anger, bitterness, aggression, control and many more.

Perhaps the greatest barrier of all is 'fear'. It controls everything beneath it. It seeps into every decision and every projection. It dominates and, worse still, let loose, it grows.

Unfortunately, fear is often a consequence of phobia and, if you're trying to sell against a hidden phobia, you have no chance. Of course, the problem with phobias is they're not real – but try telling that to the sufferer.

In our daily working life, we meet fear every day. Fear of the boss, of presenting, of failure, of others, of ourselves – the list goes on. Like well-hidden land mines, fears are destructive but it's generally too late when you see that for yourself.

There are enough stories to fill another book on emotional management and emotional decisions but that's for another day. In this, and the next chapter, these true, short stories will give you a little insight into how emotions can get in the way of business.

But first, a story about how fear became an opportunity. After all, the role of a great salesperson is to provide something that the customer doesn't yet have to allow him do what he needs or wants to do.

"Those Dogs Frighten Me"

If you are lucky, you get to work with some very interesting, charismatic and good people. I'm lucky, I can think of quite a few.

This story is about emotions and how it created opportunity. Opportunity is different to exploitation. Great sales people see opportunity and see what's fair. Bad sales people seek to exploit for their own personal gain and call it 'opportunity'.

Andrew is one of those few charismatic people who leave a deep mark, a deep good mark. Again, a recurring theme in this book, it is that rare combination of their charisma, values, attitude and sheer goodness. In my lifetime of meeting many people, Andrew stands at the very top of the most impressive. Everything that's good about Andrew is about him being good with people and good to people. He learnt the hard way.

Some time back, we were both giving a short talk to some students on the verge of finishing school. Between us, we decided to tell stories, our own stories. After all, just like those in this book, they are what we relate to.

When it came to his turn to talk, one of his compelling stories was about emotions, opportunity, courage and selling.

Andrew's dad had a friend who delivered and sold coal in an era when that was our common home heating fuel. The delivery trucks, crewed by men with muscle and blackened faces, were a common sight in days gone by. It was also an era of trust, honesty and integrity. You got the goods first and paid later. Up early every day, Andrew did newspaper rounds, milk rounds and everything necessary to fund his innocent pleasures. It was his introduction to early mornings, hard work and rewarding pastimes.

One day, Andrew's dad's friend, the coal man, confessed to being afraid of dogs. His daily rounds to collect money were tortured and made him anxious. A fear was ruling his world and this fear was very much in charge. Andrew overheard this hulk of a man confessing his fear to his dad. It had serious implications on sales and on collecting money. Fear ruled. The dogs were a threat, a barrier and a big problem.

Not for Andrew. He loved dogs. The big problem was no problem. Quick as you like, Andrew offered to ride shotgun and to collect the money from houses with dogs. The coal man was pleased and relieved.

"Really? Will you?", asked the coal man. "That would be great."

Andrew hadn't finished. He added, "It's a pleasure and I'm very happy to help you for a small additional charge for every debt that I collect".

The deal was done.

Importantly, both Andrew and the coal man got what they wanted. What Andrew saw was not really profit, opportunity or money. Andrew understood that how and why we buy often may be a consequence of our emotions as well as our logic. For the coal man and for Andrew, it was a good deal since both sides got what they wanted.

Understanding people is a complex business. Expecting people to be logical is a little like expecting a machine to cry.

But when I look back at all the characters I've encountered on my journey, I can see a rainbow of motivations. Motivation is the hidden layer that lies behind our own personal emotion or conflict. Emotions are hard to ignore and applying logic to illogical emotions is doomed to fail.

Great sales people find out what the customer's emotions and motivations are. They don't assume.

Poor sales people make assumptions and, inevitably, they are wrong. Life is never that simple.

Here are three short stories that tell you a little about emotions getting in the way of a sale. All simple, all real but each left a profound footprint.

She Froze

Miriam came across really well at the interview. Bright, professional, clear and engaging. No amount of probing or testing could derail this impressive girl. She waltzed through the questions and dodged tricky ones with skill. She got the job.

The customer was exceptionally demanding, to which was added a double-sized dollop of arrogance. Where possible, he would loudly proclaim that it was "my business". It wasn't, it was Daddy's but everyone indulged him because they were afraid. The ego reigned supreme.

He was throwing his weight around and Miriam was beginning to rock. Sensing her fear, he ramped up the pressure and launched his ear-bursting assault. She went from fear to disbelief to paralysis. He bit harder. When the slaughter was finished, she shook with fright.

No words could console her. The shock was extreme. Trauma doesn't forget. Soon after his vicious attack, Miriam resigned.

The story didn't end there. She didn't just resign. She stopped work for good, her confidence gone. The young man who carried out the attack probably will never know his impact or his legacy. It brought me back to schooldays.

When I was about 14, I had a teacher who was the epitome of calm and kindness. His name was Frank. One day, he stumbled upon a weak boy who was being bullied by a giant of an idiot. He intervened. His words never left me. I could apply them to the young man who didn't really own "my business".

He said to the bully: "It's easy to hit a sinking ship. Why don't you pick on me?".

The bully burst into tears yet Frank, in his deep kindness, consoled him. You see, there's a difference between doing what's right and feeling the need to win. Frank was wise enough to teach that to very young kids, even though it wasn't on the curriculum.

"I Won't Join You"

It's easy to throw money at problems, not so easy to make time. It might signal disinterest, dislike or simply a little inconvenient disruption. Throwing money at problems usually doesn't stick.

John was a young manager who got promoted too quickly. It went to his head. His attitude changed and he believed he could walk on water. He tried – and often sank. His arrogance was almost funny. It was swashbuckling and led to ridicule more than fear. His team were afraid of him and that suited John. He wanted them 'straightened out' and that was fair enough. They needed to confront and fix their own problems. Once done, they could plough on to a better and more efficient future.

We started early. John, attired in an immaculate Savile Row suit, met me 10 minutes before the start. I could see why he had achieved early promotion – that was then.

He came in to the class and gave a motivational pep talk. It was good, rousing and rallying. He immediately burst his own balloon with these simple words: "I won't be joining you". It was something like the captain of a transatlantic airliner saying, "Have a nice flight, I won't be with you". At least, airplanes have autopilots that aren't so sensitive.

After a low morale start, we went ahead and made great strides.

At lunchtime, John wanted an update. Letting my own emotions intrude, I said in thinly-disguised sarcastic tones: "You'd have to join us to get that answer".

At 2pm, he did just that. The mood in the room darkened. You see, the biggest problem was John. John was a bully. He was the barrier to success. Deep down, he knew it.

That night, in the bar, he asked me a very direct question. He knew he was taking a risk – so did I.

"Conor, be honest, what's the barrier that's holding them back?", came the question in a whisper.

I asked him if he wanted my opinion or what he wanted to hear. He chose the former.

I immediately said just one word, "You".

He walked away slowly. He walked in a very long, slow, wide circle, processing what I had just said.

He came back with one more question: "Are you saying I'm a bully?".

I said, "Yes".

He took off for a second slow circle, landing back in front of me.

"Are you really saying I'm a bully?"

I said, "My answer is still the same".

We went on to enjoy a wonderful night.

The next day, the bully had gone and a more modest man appeared. He joined in, ate humble pie and went on to realise his vast potential. John had enough common-sense to realise that his own self-indulgence would soon cause his own self-destruction. He came away a much better manager and a much better man.

The Secret Agent

Every conversation with Theo was in whispers. Nothing was to be overheard. It became the norm, as did his opening reply to almost everything, "Yes, but the problem with that is". Psychologists call it 'trouble-spotting'.

Theo was clandestine about everything. He worked on the basis that everything and everybody was bugged. He trusted nobody. His emotional conditioning wouldn't even allow him to join his colleagues for lunch. They might get too close. Everything was to be in secret.

He inherited really good people. They had initiative, drive and a desire to be successful. They were used to Theo saying, "I'll let you work on without me, I'll only get in the way". It was a constant cop out – they knew it too.

When the day was done, we were all tired. The reward was a sturdy piece of work that would bear fruit for many years. It was satisfying.

Around 8pm that night, Theo called me. Even though there were just the two of us, and there were no indications that the phone was bugged, he still whispered.

His first question knocked me back: "Who should I be worried about after today, Conor? Who is the threat within?".

I stumbled and instinctively said: "No one. They were superb, really good. I'd tell you if I had a concern. I don't really understand why you're asking me that question".

"Fine, fine", he said impatiently, "but who is the dark destroyer?".

I was thinking Star Wars. I thought he was joking.

The call rambled for 30 minutes. He was trouble-spotting and paranoid too. No matter what comfort I gave him that there was no conspiracy, I'll never forget his final words: "I'll prove you wrong. I don't trust them. They're up to something. When I find out, I'll call you".

He never did call me. He was transferred shortly after.

It would be all too easy to 'judge' these three people. Don't.

That's not what this chapter is about. These are stories about human frailty and how emotions can wreck decision-making, logic and common-sense. All of us, in some way, have been the victim of our own thinking, insecurity, phobia or fear. Really clever salespeople accept that and find a way around it. Actors are even better, they go into the character and never let their true weaknesses affect their role.

What have these stories got to do with selling?

A lot. People buy from people. We often see what they didn't say and hear what they didn't think we saw.

Great salespeople use a combination of the art and the science. They switch instinctively from fact to emotion, from logic to mood, and from language to body language. It's not easy to teach but it's easy to understand.

If you want to sell more, you need to listen and not hear. You need to study, not judge. You need to read, not predict and you need to understand emotions and how they drive decision-making.

Each of the three stories above has a simple moral. That is, logic and common-sense had nothing to do with the person's decision-making. Applying logic to manage any of these situations would have been useless. Each of the people described were not just driven by their emotions, they were overruled by them. When that happens, control, in every way, is lost. After that, it's only a question of 'how long?' before they crash. All three eventually did fall from high office and there, but for the grace of God, go all of us.

To succeed in selling, you must understand emotions. After all, they differentiate us from machines and nothing, but nothing, sells more effectively than people.

CHAPTER 9
CUSTOMERS

This is what customers pay us for - to sweat all these details so it's easy and pleasant for them to use our computers. We're supposed to be really good at this. That doesn't mean we don't listen to customers, but it's hard for them to tell you what they want when they've never seen anything remotely like it.
Steve Jobs

This is the philosophy that took a still young company into a global brand. Steve Jobs understood disrupting the market, brands and creating customers. Sadly, too many people in sales take a different approach – if you like, an indifferent approach. As J.K. Rowling said, "Indifference and neglect often do much more damage than outright dislike".

The Silent Exit

"Get a customer, just get one. At any cost, just bleep get one. Tell them what they want to hear. Lie if you have to and whilst you're at it, sell them the sun, moon and stars. They're just bleep customers. Who cares?"

He was a big guy. Whilst he kept me waiting, he was marking his territory, prowling, stalking and growling. I was meant to be impressed, intimidated or both. I was none of them. My blood was rising.

"Now, Kenny, what you'll do for me is this."

I had driven many miles to suffer the darkness of this man, his business and his grotesque attitude. My blood pressure rose higher.

Here was a man who bulldozed his way to big profits. He got into full flow: "You'll take my team and sort them out. Get rid of the lazy ones and let me know if there's any talent I can squeeze".

My limit had been reached. I stood up. He never noticed. I packed my bag and put on my coat. He still didn't notice. He kept talking, utterly seduced by his own words. My last glance backwards saw him speaking faster with eyes fixed on the ceiling, his thoughts all-consuming. He was intoxicated by his own demons. I closed the door behind me. He never even noticed.

This was a customer I didn't ever want and I have never regretted saying 'No' to the wrong customer. If you don't, they will destroy your business, your sanity and your team.

Sometimes, saying 'No' is simply the only option, the brave option and the right option.

Peter Drucker said: *"The purpose of a business is to create a customer"*. The opposite is probably to create enemies.

Good Customers

It would be difficult to pick out the very many good customers I've had the pleasure to work with over the years but there are many. Each has a unique character, combined with absolute integrity. In short, they are good people who bring their integrity to work.

Good customers have many similar traits. Here are the common denominators that I have seen:

- They are not just good customers, they are also good employers. They don't separate people into types.
- They have integrity and a deep understanding of being fair.
- They are committed to excellence, learning and sharing wisdom.
- They understand the imperfections of humans.
- They have charisma, personality and warmth.
- They are honest and confident.
- They know what they don't know. They seek help where there's a knowledge gap.
- They value expertise.
- They have a clear vision.
- They are usually successful and understated.
- They are cheerful, optimistic and positive.
- They do good things for people outside their work.

- They are accessible.
- They do business rather than winning or losing.
- They listen.
- They are humble.

Bad Customers

Part of the journey to successful selling is the inevitable sleepless nights caused by bad customers. They consume your thinking, your time and your business. They are no good to you and 'business at all costs' is a very dangerous strategy. I have encountered my fair share and the short stories in this chapter tell their own tale.

What common traits dominate their thinking? I can't answer scientifically but I can tell you what I saw:

- They value profit over people.
- They seek personal gain rather than the greater good.
- They are troubled.
- They are insecure.
- They are under pressure.
- They have ego.
- They are not happy.
- They have a warped set of values.
- They don't trust.
- They can be paranoid.
- They have little integrity.
- They insult others.
- They are not positive or cheerful.
- They are selfish.
- They are insatiable.
- They don't respect external advice and expertise.
- They begrudge having to work with you.
- They lose staff frequently.

- They are pirates.

Bad Customer Care

It's hard enough to attract attention, let alone make a sale. Strangely enough, some sales people seem to spend their life avoiding customers, opportunities and even sales.

Just as I began the first tentative steps in writing this book, a gift appeared out of the blue – a story that you wouldn't ordinarily believe – one that convinced me to keep on writing.

It was mid-afternoon and I was in the middle of meeting an article deadline that needed my attention. I was working from home, a rare treat on a winter's day. In a smartphone world, I was surprised by the ringing from my trusty old and virtually redundant landline.

"Shall I answer it and break my train of thought?"

Curiosity got the better of me. I did. I'm glad I did.

It was a 'customer service call' from my landline provider. I'd been with them forever. In today's competitive telecoms world, they had to work harder. But, old habits die hard. I was intrigued as the carefully-scripted, cliché-ridden call began.

"Good afternoon, this is Joe from Customer Care".

His dead tones said he didn't.

"I'm just calling to check that everything is all right and you are happy with everything?"

I think he was terrified I might say *No.*

I've always admired anyone who can work in a call centre. It's tough. Lots of repetition mixed in with a lot of rejection. I'm sure they don't like Mondays. I was gentle but firm.

"Thanks for calling me, Joe. Now that I have you, come to think of it, my broadband speed has been very poor lately."

There was a long pause – a very long pause. The script hadn't anticipated this one. Paralysis set in. Joe cleared his throat unconvincingly.

With indecent haste, he said: "Your broadband is slow? You'll have to ring in about that. I'm only Customer Care".

Before I had time to say another word, Joe said, "Good afternoon", and hung up.

I couldn't stop smiling. Joe had just kick-started a slow news day.

Mr Motivator

If I read the following story in a book, I wouldn't believe it. When I heard it, I had to check with a colleague that he had said what I thought he had said. He had.

Business was tough and fear ran through the company. It was easy to see. Hurried walks as close to the corridor wall as you could get. False thin smiles that were simply scary and *"I wouldn't know"* the safe default answer to any question that might have a hint of controversy. It was a bleak atmosphere that added to a bleak economy.

We worked away and met up with some lieutenants for lunch. It was a solemn affair. Downcast faces ate for the sake of it because The Boss projected subtle threats to anyone not laughing at his wisecracks or humour. As soon as anyone was brave enough to join the conversation, he cut across them with incredible speed. They had seen it all before and never came back for more.

He dominated lunch. Then again, he dominated everything. He must have feared their views to have developed such accurate and well-timed interventions. It was almost an art.

Every chance he got, he turned the conversation to money, cutbacks and pressure. He rattled the 'We need more sales' bucket to the point where their food was abandoned. He raised the temperature at every turn. Eventually, numbed by the incessant message, they just slumped in submission. He seemed pleased and we noticed his rising good humour.

The uncomfortable pause was embarrassing. The half-eaten food was the perfect prop. Everyone was low except for Mr Motivator. Sensing another chance to 'impress', he saved his best missile until last. It was incredible.

"Did I tell you about my new sports car, folks? It's the business."

Our mouths fell awkwardly open and our eyes rolled.

His own team said nothing. They'd been here before.

"Let's Get More Out of Them"

It's hard not to take an instant like or dislike to some people. Sometimes, when you look back, it was a tiny thing that made you think, *"I'm not sure I really like this chap"* or, more importantly, *"I'm not sure if his business is good for our business"*.

We had travelled a long way to meet Michael. Our task would take all day. That was fine. We arrived early just before 9am with three hours already done. We had to leave at 6pm: a train wouldn't wait.

The meeting room was cold and the atmosphere matched the temperature – but off we went.

His team were local and appeared loyal. They were warm and charming but their future, as we soon discovered, would not be there. With hindsight, we were not surprised.

We worked hard, all of us.

Lunchtime came and the small airless room demanded a break. It didn't come. Under no circumstances was Michael going to use up precious and 'expensive' time on the folly of food. He had anticipated the desire to break.

The sandwiches arrived looking cold and worn. A quarter sandwich for everyone. Surely this was a plate for one? It wasn't; it was a plate for six.

We worked on, as his team wilted. He woke them from their semi-stupor with a battle cry of "Only two hours left, folks. Stay alert".

We stayed alert, we were used to this. His team were fading fast, very fast.

At 5:52pm, I thought we were done. Nine solid hours and a huge amount achieved. His team thought we were done too and, as if the final whistle had blown, they headed for the warm comfort off the pitch.

The shrill of his 'whistle' had other ideas. These were his very words: "Hang on, folks, come back. These guys are expensive. We have six minutes left. Let's get more out of them".

It's something you might 'think' to yourself but not something you'd actually say.

I had to check that I wasn't dreaming. I wasn't.

He got those precious six minutes that day – but he got more too. Within a very short space of time, his lieutenants had deserted and we did too. His six minutes cost him a lifetime of no going back.

CHAPTER 10
SELL THE PROBLEM

We cannot solve our problems with the same thinking we used when we created them.
Albert Einstein

Look out your office window or from your car when you're driving to or from work. How many signs say some variation on *"We sell solutions"*.

Lots perhaps?

Don't, don't sell the solution. Sell the problem first.

Let me explain: first, the wrong way to do it; then the right way.

My Dentist

I have the world's best dentist. His name is Denis. He has the world's best gatekeeper, her name is Phil. They exude expertise, professionalism, warmth and integrity. I never want to go to another dentist.

But once, in London, a piercing toothache wouldn't wait. So I found a local solution. He was just down the road.

"Could I come at 3pm?", I asked.

"Of course, any time this afternoon will be fine."

That should have been warning enough. Good dentists don't have many free slots.

I was immediately stuck by how young he was. The medical gown looked more like something he'd wear at a fancy dress party. Little things that were painless with Denis were now challenging. I heard *"Sorry"* too much for comfort.

Post-treatment, the young dentist started selling: "You need two of these and one of those. Also, you might consider one of these and a bit of this, that and the other".

My alarm bells rang. Denis had never seen such a destroyed set of teeth. I was suspicious and I wasn't having any of it.

A month later, I went for a check-up from my own trusty friend. I said little and waited for the assessment.

"Your teeth are perfect, Conor. See you in a year."

"So, Denis, I don't need a, b, c and d?", I asked.

"Of course not. Why are you asking?", came the slightly confused reply.

"Oh, I was just wondering. Nothing more."

I always look forward to visiting the dentist. My dentist, not any other dentist. Trying to over-sell the problem is a quick road to quicksand.

My Painter

There are people who do what they do because it is who they are. Think of a kindly doctor, nurse or friend. Then, there are those who do what they do purely to fill their personal money-tank and nothing else. With experience, it's easy to see the difference.

Alan came to look at the house. It was time to freshen up, repaint and look smart. No, I couldn't have a price until Alan had a good look. He wanted to be accurate and, even though it was costing him time, he didn't want to take a wild guess at the cost. I admired his patience and his concern to do things properly.

On time, Alan arrived. He was cheerful, relaxed and his perfectly branded clothing exuded professionalism. He had two fellows with him. Big excitement when he revealed the two to be brothers; that took at least five minutes of discussion and celebration. I'm not sure why – but it did.

All three went to different parts of the house to assess the work to be done. They took notes and seemed in no rush even though it was 7pm on a beautiful summer Friday evening. They must have been there an hour. Not together in some secret discussion, but earnestly making notes. When they finished, there was no instant price. They needed to assess all the notes. Alan would come back the next day.

He did and the brothers too. The conversation went something like this: "Everything is in very good condition and we don't need to do some of the areas you asked us to do. It would be a waste of money. Also, if we use this paint, it's better than the one you suggested and we will save you lots of unnecessary outlay. Can we also do the skirting boards in the downstairs rooms? They need attention. Finally, the garden shed and deck really need attention, so we will do all that too".

The last piece was interesting. He sold the problem – the shed. He didn't say what it would cost or what the problem was. It just needed 'attention'.

It's easy to be suspicious and I can hear your question: "Did he charge you much more for doing the shed?". The answer is *No*.

Of course, they got the job.

Alan and the two brothers probably don't even realise they sold the problem. They were honest, cheerful, reasonable and sincere. They did really good work, with incredible attention to detail. They made the shed look new and the deck the same. Yes, they sold the problem but they delivered a great solution – and that's what brings you back again and again.

A week or two later, I went up to my shiny, newly-painted shed. As I reached for the door-handle, I sighed. I knew the shed was in a bit of a mess, and that I'd have to pull, tug and heave to get what I wanted.

I didn't. Without saying a word, Alan and the two brothers hadn't just painted the shed, they'd tidied it too. And not just tidied it, but tidied it immaculately.

No wonder I had to wait to get them. I'll wait the next time too.

CHAPTER 11
WHY SHOULD I BUY FROM YOU?

In making a speech one must study three points: first, the means of producing persuasion; second, the language; third, the proper arrangement of the various parts of the speech.
Aristotle

The only real question your customer wants to know the answer to – although, funnily enough, they won't mention it – is: *"Why should I buy from you?"*.

If you struggle to answer it, then you are facing an uphill battle.

Of course, the reality is that many sales people are really asking this question of their potential customer: *"What can you do to help me reach my target, bonus or commission?"*.

A good buyer will have lots of fun tying you up in knots as soon as they spot your selfish mission and purpose. They will see the thinly veiled truth faster than you think.

To get it right as to why they should buy from you, think about an answer that begins with: *"Because A, B, C …"*. In fact, you should be able to fire out five or six *"Because …"* statements, without thinking.

When you do, think of these little pointers:

- Avoid evocative words such as 'magical experiences' or 'amazing people';
- Make sure you know how the feature you describe benefits the customer (not you);
- Be clear that these are unique selling points *versus* your competitor(s);
- Understand why they are unique selling points;
- Be clear about your mission and purpose at your meeting;
- Know your brand;

- Know your message;
- Know what your customer needs;
- Understand his / her buying motives;
- Understand him / her;
- Understand what motivates him / her;
- Understand that what you think is not what you know.

Here are some true stories that will tell you more about why people sold and why they didn't sell. I seem to appear in both.

The Best-dressed Man

I remember going on lots of sales courses in my earlier career. Most were of little value. Many were academic, some were theoretical and most were just far too abstract. I often left feeling that they had made something that should be simple into something else much too complicated. Sometimes, these sales courses were just rewoven versions of the same formula thinly disguised as original content. The best lessons are always simple moments, simple statements at a time when you're ready to receive them.

Phil was my boss. He was patient, calm and wise, an all-round nice guy. But it wasn't these qualities that made an impact – it was how Phil dressed.

He was always immaculately groomed, elegant, fashionable and just cool. He was understated but his sense of style gave him a charisma and presence you don't often see. It wasn't long before others took notice.

Phil came to work one morning and told me he was jumping ship. He was moving, not just to a better job but to a superb job. To be honest, I was a little surprised at his quantum leap. It turned out he was just as surprised.

We talked about his impending move and I was keen to know how he had managed to land such fantastic high office. We chatted back and forth but it was his final sentence that really struck me: "You know what they said after I'd been offered the job? They said that part of the reason I got it was because 'I looked successful'".

He was absolutely right. He did.

Seduction and the First Date

Selling is no different to the noble art of seduction.

First, you have to make someone aware that you exist. You have to get noticed.

Once you get noticed, you have to be a different option to everyone else. Imagine if everyone in the bar looked exactly the same? Then, an hour later, the door opened again and in came more clones? Hardly an exciting night full of possibility.

But if someone a little different came in, then you'd notice them. It might be their clothes, their hair, their attitude or even their charisma. But, they wouldn't be more of the same, they would stand out. That's why you'd notice them.

Again, the greatest single mistake marketing people make is that they can't answer the question customers ask but never say: *"Why should I buy from you?"*.

It sounds simple but it's not. It's especially difficult when you are competing in a sea full of like for like products. I know, I was there.

The School Photo

Some years back, in a very old and battle-worn scrapbook, I found a photo of my final year class at school. You know the type: a row at the front, a few well-balanced benches rising to four tiers of agitated restless schoolboys.

It was beautifully set up. The ornate school door was the backdrop, well balanced by strong granite pillars.

Row one were perfect. Sitting tightly together, hands outstretched and fresh-faced young cheeks.

Row two was even better, they were standing. Like soldiers, they stood proud, chests out and heads held high.

Row three was a problem. The perfect picture was almost perfect – but not quite. At the very end of row three was my lifelong friend, Vincent.

Vincent was never a man to conform. Never a man to do the easy thing. Always a man who chose a different path.

Just as the photo was to be taken, I noticed Vincent was shuffling. At the very moment of the photo, Vincent moved a foot away from me. I was a little perplexed and even more so when he said, "Perfect timing".

A few years later, we were looking back over some photos from our days in boarding school. I clearly remembered his agitated state that day. I asked him about it. His response was his normal response: he just laughed. Then, turning to our class photo, he said: "What do you notice about the photo?".

I said, "It's perfectly posed and perfectly lined up but there's a big gap between you and me which wrecked the balance of the image".

Again, he just laughed.

"You see, my dear friend, you missed the point. I didn't want it to be a perfect photo where I just blended in. I wanted to be different. I wanted to be noticed. I wanted to be me. If I had allowed myself to stand tight beside you, you'd never have noticed me but you did. You see, Conor, I always like to stand out from the crowd".

He did and he continues to do so.

If you want to get noticed, isn't that one of the very first things you have to do? Blending in is zoning out.

The House on the Hill

A few years ago, I was giving a workshop. I knew that I would struggle to really explain the difference between being a regular sales person *versus* an exceptional one (you know the type? The one who stands out from the crowd) so, rather than offload lots of theory, I told a story. It goes something like this.

There was a very rich man who lived in a very big house, high on the hill. His name was Mr Timmins. Mr Timmins was very wealthy and owned lots of different businesses locally. He was a very well-fed sort of chap with a hearty laugh. His suits were three-piece and his sparkling pocket-watch was a symbol of success. He was kind but he was also tough. If you presented a good argument, you would write lots of orders. If you didn't, you would leave empty handed.

Every Friday, Mr Timmins would grant all the sales people a short audience. His house was clearly visible from the road and, every Friday, its perfectly manicured winding driveway was streaming with sales people going up or coming away. Outside his house, the leafy country road was packed with sales reps' cars.

Annabel was a very clever girl. A great listener, very patient and above all, a great observer. She had driven here before to see how Friday went – she was smart enough not to rush in. She knew the difference between urgent and important.

Annabel quickly spotted something: all the sales people drove the same cars, even the colours were the same. They all wore ill-fitting suits and dull grey ties. They were reasonably cheerful going towards the house and empty-handed and miserable coming back down the drive. At the big gold and black gates, they looked impatient waiting to be let in as if they already knew their fate. Annabel knew this needed fresh thinking, new ideas and a different approach.

The following Wednesday, when nobody was around, Annabel decided to wander up the road behind the house. The big black and gold gates were firmly locked, it wasn't Friday after all. But it was worth doing some research.

A bumpy unused road led to the back of Mr Timmins' enormous immaculate house. To her surprise, there was only a low wall with a low little gate. The gate was open, so Annabel peered in. Singing softly in the garden was a friendly looking lady who also seemed fond of life's edible treats. She spotted Annabel and said, "Come in, my dear, come in. You must see my roses". In no time, they were deep in conversation about gardens, flowers and the beauty of the countryside. That led to home-made cookies and the finest tea in the finest china.

Never one to miss a treat, who should pop his portly frame into the kitchen only Mr Timmins. His immaculate three-piece suit had surrendered to a collarless white shirt and big red braces. A man who cut a dash, even when relaxing. His welcome was warm and his and his wife's goodness overflowing.

Before long, it was time to go. As Annabel was leaving, Mr Timmins came with her to her car.

"I never asked you what you do for a living, Annabel. My deepest apology. I'm so rude. I was completely caught up in our wonderful chat about gardens, roses and life".

As patient as ever, Annabel smiled and said, "I'm in sales".

Mr Timmins smiled broadly.

"I love sales people. I admire them but, sadly, many don't want to be in sales or even like their job. Anyway, enough of that, my dear. Now I must tell you that every Friday I love to meet sales people and I adore cheering up their Friday by giving them lots of orders."

Annabel smiled knowingly but kept her counsel.

"Now then, as a good friend of Mrs Timmins, you must come next Friday and maybe I can give you some business. Wouldn't that make a great start to your weekend, Annabel, wouldn't it?"

Annabel smiled again but said nothing. You see, Mr Timmins liked to talk.

"Oh dear, silly me", said Mr Timmins. "Fridays can be so very busy, you know. Cars come and block up our little winding road. They get angry and start blowing the horn and they even fight a little amongst themselves. It can be wearing. I'll tell you what, Annabel, I open the gates for appointments at noon. Why don't you come at 11 and, this time, pop in the back door? After we have talked business, we can have more tea. Now off with you and promise me you won't tell anyone about our back gate?"

Once more, Annabel smiled and said, "I'll see you at 11".

They both smiled and a relationship was born.

The Pen

I was beginning to admire myself and maybe even dispense a well-earned pat or two on my own back. Months of negotiation finally had led to the dramatic climax of contracts being signed. It had been a tricky road but success was in reach. Just 'dot the i's and cross the t's'. The rewards were rich. The buyer was a well-worn man. In the twilight of his career, he had seen it all. He watched my every move but I had successfully jumped every hurdle. So I thought.

It was time to sign. In my haste, I produced my pen, eager for closure and the end.

In seconds, I'd noticed his laser-like stare. My pen was a cheap, well-worn, well-chewed ordinary ballpoint pen. He looked disgusted, because he was.

"You want me to sign a contract for thousands and thousands? You expect me to sign it with that pen? Get out of here."

I was devastated and shocked. My head was spinning wildly. In a blur, I went to the elevator, not even sure where I was going. All was lost. The sale, my target, my commission and, more importantly, my self-respect.

I got to the large tomb-like reception area where the smiling receptionist reminded me that I had to return my pass. Handing it over, I turned to leave. Just then, the smiling receptionist held a telephone out to me, saying, "Hold on, Mr Smith in purchasing wants a word".

I took the telephone, hands trembling. He summoned me back to the 19th floor.

"Conor, never ever ask someone to sign a huge contract with a cheap, nasty, unclean pen. You are getting the contract but I wanted you to learn something about selling, not just for today but forever."

All these years later, in this book, Mr Smith's precious wisdom is still alive. Now you know why I have a thing about nice pens.

"You're Giving Me a Headache"

Sales people have a wonderful capacity for winging it. I know, I tried it too.

Like the pirate, you might get away with it once or twice but my bet is you'll perish on the high seas. Really good selling means you must know what you're talking about. If you don't, you cannot succeed.

Worse still is the salesman who talks too much. I know, I did too.

At long last, I'd managed to secure a meeting with the buyer of a very big company. He was a gruff man who didn't like his job very much. He liked sales people even less.

When I entered his airless office, he greeted me with a scowl. His feet rested on the well-worn desk and he was mentally in a permanent hangover.

On the side of his desk was a huge clock, complete with oversized alarm bells. He set the alarm for 10 minutes hence. I was already on the back foot. Looking at me with utter disdain, he said, "You've 10 minutes to sell me your stuff. Go!".

Nerves got the better of me and I rushed, rambled and skidded wildly. After about five minutes, he shouted at me, "Stop".

I stopped.

"You're giving me a headache. Get out of my office."

Drained and distressed, I left empty-handed. I took the lift and wandered the busy street outside in a daze. It wasn't so much the failed sale as the scolding. I was angry and confused.

Over time, I recovered. He was right. I talked too much. I rambled. I didn't know my product and didn't know my audience. I wasn't prepared and I thought I'd 'talk' my way to a sale. Those few minutes of terror taught me some very powerful lessons. If you don't prepare, you prepare to fail.

More importantly, bad sales people think that the more they talk, the more they are persuading. Clever sales people know that less is more. Or, as my Dad once told me: "Say little, let them talk and they will think you're a great chap".

It reminded me of another impressive line from Stephen Covey that every sales person should remember: "Most people do not listen with the intent to understand; they listen with the intent to reply".

"Liked or Respected?"

Everybody adored William. He was a great guy: full of stories, full of fun and he knew everybody there is to know.

William also liked his glass of wine and more. He liked it so much that he spent at least eight hours a day in what he called his 'office'. It was his control tower, where everything was done.

Anytime I'd see him, he was deep in intense conversation. I marvelled at his network, contacts and contracts. I was sure William was wealthy as well as powerful. I was wrong. I was so very wrong.

Not too many years after I last met William, I learnt of his very early death. His fondness for alcohol had taken an early toll. Even sadder was the abject poverty that I now learnt to be his reality. It all began to fall into place.

You see, William made a very simple error: he confused being liked with being respected. Everybody enjoyed his company, everybody accepted his charm, stories and generosity but sadly, very few respected him professionally and his 'office' became the stick that beat him.

William was a good man but his personal compass set him on a road to ruin. William met everybody, talked a great talk, but never completed a potential sale. The bright lights of the next exciting opportunity always lured him away from completing the immediate task. For sales people, it can be a heady cocktail that completely distorts the outcome. It is tempting and it is dangerous.

Quite simply, great sales people crave respect far more than popularity. One sustains, the other destroys. It takes an inner confidence and resolve to ignore the rejection and it takes insecurity to rise above it. Your story is not who you are.

Unemployed

Everybody should experience unemployment at least once – to be kind, only for a short while. It teaches perhaps the most precious lesson of all: that we take far too much for granted and may even waste our lives dreaming of an illusionary future. When you are unemployed, you see the true worth of work. It's about a lot more than money, it's about your purpose and about who you are.

In London, I was unemployed for almost six months. I understand the slippery slope and how it poisons self-esteem, confidence and more. It's a spiral that leads to a dark deep pit. It is the enemy of a career and the enemy of living a fulfilling life. Tread carefully when you talk with someone in this situation; they are already well down the ladder of life, hope and esteem. But, like any unpleasant adventure, you can emerge wiser if you accept the arduous lesson.

Early each morning, before today's online world, I walked to the newsagent to buy the daily paper. Eagerly, I would scour every advert and enthusiastically reply in search of work. There was a deep recession and jobs were scarce but I would keep climbing. I didn't like the alternative nasty fall into the deep, dark well. I had sent over 200 handwritten letters. I received only eight replies. Eventually, rejection takes its toll, you lose hope and your meagre savings erode fast. It's a lousy lesson and hard to see beyond.

Life's most defining moments are simple, incredibly simple. There's no crash of thunder, oceans parting or bright white light. They are random moments when, deep down in your consciousness, you are ready to receive the new wisdom.

My moment was simple. It was my usual walk to the newsagent and a beautiful busy spring morning. Suburban London was shaking off sleep and cranking up for a busy day. The rush hour traffic into the city was its usual heavy self but that's not what caught my eye. The big shiny red London bus was gliding very slowly in front of me nose to tail in rush-hour traffic. The passengers were packed tight and I envied every single one of them, they were going to work. I longed to be squashed on that London bus. They had a destination, I had none.

I looked closer and studied their faces carefully. Every face looked miserable, unhappy and depressed. I couldn't understand it. They just didn't get it. They were lucky, though I bet they looked at me thinking how 'lucky' I was to be 'off' in the spring air. First impressions can be so misleading.

I walked home, head a little low. In the front door I went, to find a letter on the doormat. Hope, excitement and a little anxiety. The letter said my résumé was interesting and they'd like to talk to me. It came from the boss and even gave me a time and his private direct line. I was overjoyed.

Nervous, excited and with a fast-beating heart, I called at 3pm precisely. It was time to make the ultimate sale, the sale of myself.

It started well and I was soon on a roll. Confidence growing, I kept talking. In hindsight, that looks more like 'talking and talking and talking'. Nervous excitement can destroy a sale.

Mid-sentence, if not mid-word, he had enough. The decision was made. He had reached a conclusion. In dull, tired tones and a small hint of distaste, he said: "I won't delay you any further".

The phone went dead. I thought I might follow suit.

Yes, I'd made an impact alright, it just happened to be the wrong one.

CHAPTER 12
GATEKEEPERS

Great spirits have always encountered violent opposition from mediocre minds.
Albert Einstein

In your passionate sales mind, it is utterly stupid for the customer to do anything other than to meet you.

Why wouldn't anyone want to? *Of course,* they need to see your product and buy from you. Obvious if they want to get all the benefits. Right?

Reality might be different. There are always 'gatekeepers', whose job is to keep you out at all costs. You can appeal to their sense of reason, commercial integrity and more – but you'll just waste time. Some gatekeepers thrive on being the immovable barrier.

In selling, running like a bull at a heavy steel gate and hoping it will eventually open is foolish. Strangely, many sales people keep applying the same tactic and are surprised when they always get the same result.

Clever sales people acknowledge the gate and plot their way around it.

Claire with an I

You could see her bright red lipstick from 100 paces. If you looked closely, you'd know that her every last cent was spent on preserving youth. I could only wonder at how many hours went into the daily ritual to get ready to set sail on a long commute to London's West End.

Her desk was 'her' desk. It wrapped around her like a giant hug. In every way, it was as immaculate as her own personal deportment. Everything was in order. To the left, a flashing, twinkling array of colourful lights. To her right, papers, forms and passes. The centre of the desk was the centre of her world, Claire with an I's world.

Her sturdy arms skilfully juggled the lights, the forms and the chewing gum that occasionally flashed the whitest teeth you've ever seen. Even her glasses formed part of the kit. In fact, everything seemed connected, except perhaps her approach.

Phone calls were an inconvenience and triggered an eye-roll. Waiting visitors were welcomed in a cold, 'eye you up and down' way. Salesmen came – and went.

They tried charm, seduction, flattery and aggression. They failed to make a scratch. Claire with an I was not for turning.

"No appointment, No Go. Vamoose."

Grown men wept. They vamoosed, empty-handed.

In between vamooses, Claire liked to chat to her friends in an indiscreet sort of way, "So Caroline, back to Saturday night, it was just amaaaaazing". We knew her Saturday night was probably a little more sedate, but we smiled in the hope that her heart might melt and we would be admitted into the Buyer's Office. We weren't.

I knew that a standard approach would end in "Vamoose". I wasn't about to head into a cul-de-sac so I left without saying a word. I'd live to fight another day.

As I was walking out the door, in a loud, excited voice, Claire with an I said to her telephone friend, "I Love Turkish Delight. Oh my God, I just LOVE it". We didn't doubt her.

Sales were bad and I was looking into a grim future. If only Claire with an I would let me in to meet Maggie, the buyer, I'd be saved.

I found myself in a newsagent. As if by divine intervention, an enormous colourful box of Turkish Delight gazed down on me. I'm convinced it winked. It cost £8 and I had £10 to last me the rest of the week. It was a big gamble but a bleak sales wasteland wasn't especially inviting either. Biting the bullet, I bought the box. In for a penny, in for a pound.

A deep breath, as big a smile as I could manufacture and an iron will, I walked straight at Claire's world. The default snarl widened a little, her eyes drawn to the magic box. The chewing gum stopped.

"Good afternoon, Claire", I said in as confident and sincere a voice as I could muster. "For you, to thank you for all your help in the past."

Claire looked confused and bewildered but went with it because the Turkish Delight was hypnotising.

"You're very welcome", she said, eyes fixed on her prize.

"I know it's late, but do you think Maggie might see me now?", I chanced.

"Of course, come on through."

I ran. Behind me, I could hear the verbal machetes from the other waiting salepeople whistling towards my back. It had taken me six months to get this far – they could say what they liked. I was in.

Claire with an I never did enquire as to how she had helped me in the past. She just assumed she had.

Maggie

As a buyer, Maggie was legendary. Get on with Maggie and you'd reach your target in one fell swoop.

Maggie knew that – so she employed Claire with an I to defend her. But, through the judicious use of some expensive Turkish Delight, I got past Claire with an I to meet Maggie.

Maggie and I got on well – very well. But no sales resulted.

I was confused. I'd conquered the hardest hill. I'd met Maggie, several times, but I wasn't selling. Where was I going wrong?

My approach had always been 'the nice guy'. No pressure, no strong arming, just be nice because it's nice to be nice. It might be 'nice' but it wasn't getting results. I'd cracked the gatekeeper, got to Maggie, built a relationship but, I wasn't selling.

One sunny summer day, I'd had another fruitless chat with Maggie. It was lunchtime and she walked out of the office with me, through the doors and out into the brilliant sunshine. Maggie was clearly in a good mood. The sun, Friday and her impending holiday collided to make this a very happy day.

Without prompting, Maggie offered: "You know, Conor, what I like about you is that you're not pushy. You don't hassle me and you're not constantly knocking on my door looking to see me and looking to sell".

Where on earth could this be going, I asked myself?

Maggie's next line hit me like a rock.

"You see, Conor, I have to deal with all these sales people all the time. They can be annoying, so annoying. Continuously calling, constantly emailing and even walking in unannounced. Oh my, they are such a persistent lot."

I waited with my mouth hanging loosely open.

"So, to get rid of them, I just give them an order or two and that gets them off my back for at least a month. It always works."

It's fine to be a nice guy but not so fine if you're not persistent. Any decision is always better than no decision and persistence pays.

Remember the word once more – persistent.

CHAPTER 13
TEAM WORK

I'm going to tell you the story about the geese which fly 5,000 miles from Canada to France. They fly in V-formation but the second ones don't fly. They're the subs for the first ones. And then the second ones take over – so it's teamwork.
Alex Ferguson

"Do you do team-building days?" came the rather rushed telephone enquiry.

"What do you mean?", I replied.

"You know, team-building days. Days where the team come back highly-motivated, energised and really up for it?"

"Up for what?", I enquired.

"You know, up for it", he said impatiently.

When he finished talking, I understood his position. I didn't agree but I understood.

As gently as I could, I told him that such days out were fun, exciting, filled with laughter, competition and even mud. I also told him that 'fun' didn't build a 'team' – only the satisfaction of hard work and a tangible achievement did.

Building a team is a complex business and it certainly doesn't happen overnight. 'Team work' is one of those clichés that everyone agrees with, but few reflect on. It's often a manager's rousing battle-cry: *"We need more team work"*. But what does that mean?

We understand teamwork easily when we watch sport. Translating that into the workplace is difficult and, in many cases, it's the 'solo runs' that win – and lose – battles.

In my daily working life, I am almost always working with teams. They are always different, though in each there's a different mix of personality, inner conflict, power, politics and personal pursuit. Often, they reflect the attitude, values and culture created by the leader.

Get it right and you'll power forward.

Get it wrong and your wheels will dig deeper into the mud as you try to accelerate out.

To explain real team-building, these two stories might help.

"It's His Business, Not Ours"

Sheila was a good girl, a very good girl. In the beginning, it didn't seem that way. Looks can be deceptive, even disinterested-looking looks.

Tom was a passionate owner, a little loud with a tendency to dive deep into somebody else's thought. It was well-intentioned but disruptive.

He started our day with a rallying call. His theme was 'teamwork'.

"We must pull together and be a real team".

I did pause to wonder what was the alternative to a 'real' team.

"It's all about team work", he kept saying.

The more he said it, the more they zoned out. As Tom took flight, they sank lower. We were heading for a wall.

Sheila broke the silence. Her pent-up passion needed to burst. It did.

"Tom, the problem here is that it's your business, not ours. That's it."

Tom smiled and his brand-new million-dollar teeth blinded us all. There was no stopping him.

"Team work, Sheila, team work. It's all about team work."

Sheila didn't even try to disguise her yawn this time.

Intervening in anyone's debate is always tricky. Like a good comedian, it's about timing. If I didn't act now, the day was lost.

"Sheila, I get you", I gently said. "Let me explain."

At this point, I had no idea how I was going to 'explain' but I was acting on instinct and in the knowledge that not intervening could only be worse than the worst intervention I could make. Diving quick and deep into my mind's pictorial archives, I needed a story and a story that would plug the widening gap.

From somewhere deep within, this is what I said, "Sheila, we are on a beach. All eight of us, including Tom. It's not a bad day and it's not a bad beach but the little island just over there is far more beautiful, sunnier, warmer and happier. If we were there, it would be much better than here. Our job, our mission, is to get there."

Sheila listened, but the curl on her lip said, "You've a long way to go to convince me, Conor".

I knew she was right.

"So we have this very pretty wooden boat that was built by true craftsmen and it is certainly the most attractive boat on the beach. We all know those admiring even slightly jealous glances from the other boat owners."

Sheila was beginning to sit up. She wasn't sure where this was going but curiosity was getting the better of her.

"This beautiful boat was built for eight people. There are seats for four to row on the starboard side and four on the port side. If all eight row together, in unison, in the same direction, we can make it to the island. If we are seven or six or less, we will struggle and probably go around in ever-decreasing circles."

I was in full flow but so too was Sheila. Perched on the very edge of her seat, Sheila wanted to finish my tale. She did, beautifully. This is what she said.

"So, Conor, Tom might be a bit of a show-off and even boast about his boat but, although he owns the boat, he won't ever make it to the island without us. In other words, without us, he has nothing, no boat, no business, no energy and no future."

All I could say was "Exactly".

Sheila got it. She was a natural leader. What did she say next?

"Tom, go get your oar, the light is fading, and you do want to get to Happy Island tonight, don't you? I do."

I smiled and left.

Tom did too. Sheila was already rowing.

'Heartbreak Hill'

Besides my work, distance running is my passion. It is full of good people, good fun and good times. It also hurts.

On Sunday mornings, we take off up the mountains to run a 10-mile route that has seen many feet over many years. It's a tough run and unforgiving. There is simply no place to hide.

Whilst runners will support you in every way, they certainly are not soft. If you can't keep up, you get dropped and 10 miles is a long lonely road without company.

I was unfit. A bout of real flu, travel and work had knocked out my rhythmic run. Still, the head never thinks the body won't keep up.

At 8am, we were off. The initial chat soon fades. People warm up and focus on personal goals. Like chess, distance running can be a game, a game where you're going to be challenged, tested and inspired.

The first real hill comes after two miles. It was designed by the Devil – personally and with malice. It is short, sharp and, no matter how often you attack it, it bites back. You recover but some start to fade.

Another long three-mile upward slope burns your legs. You keep going. This particular day, I was struggling badly at mile 5. The toughest mile had yet to come.

With 'Heartbreak Hill' in sight, I was 200 metres off the pack. My morale dipped but runners rarely quit. The hill starts gently, then growls. From a growl to a roar, it punishes your lack of fitness and, just when you think it's at its most evil, it bites again. Above all else, it's a mental battle and a solo run is confusing, isolating and bad for the soul.

I never caught up and came in four minutes (an eternity) behind. The last five miles were torture.

We went for our post-run coffee and the endorphins were flowing. My mood was not as joyous but runners are an honest lot, refreshingly so.

"You're not fit, Conor, you need to train harder."

They can be even more direct. It does you good.

An old friend turned to me, aware of my disappointment.

Brian is a good runner and a good man. He is cheerful, clear and sees everything with incredible clarity. He's the kind of guy that gives it to you straight. There's no agenda, just truth, clarity and confidence.

"We used to all be very fit, Conor. Today some are, and some are not. We used to go up that hill in a pack. Someone would lead, someone encourage and someone would tell a story. We'd focus and encourage and, before you knew it, you'd be up and over Heartbreak Hill."

I listened closely. Brian continued.

"You see, the hill is just the hill, it's no harder, and it just seems harder. When we worked together, it seemed easy. We would help, support and play our part. Today, we are running it individually and that's why it hurts. No company, no chart, no support. Isn't it just like life itself? My point, Conor? If you want to get fit and conquer big hills, then you need to work harder to stay with the pack."

That short conversation taught me more about team work than anything else, ever.

The Goose Story

How the geese cross the Atlantic together is a lesson us humans ought to grasp. They have discovered what we have not. If you haven't read the full version before (the author is unknown), here it is.

When you see geese flying along in 'V' formation, you might consider what science has discovered as to why they fly that way.

As each bird flaps its wings, it creates an uplift for the bird immediately following. By flying in 'V' formation, the whole flock adds at least 71 per cent greater flying range than if each bird flew on its own. People who share a common direction and sense of community can get where they are going more quickly and easily because they are travelling on the thrust of one another.

When a goose falls out of formation, it suddenly feels the drag and resistance of trying to go it alone — and quickly gets back into formation to take advantage of the lifting power of the bird in front. If we have as much sense as a goose, we will stay in formation with those people who are headed the same way we are.

When the lead goose gets tired, it rotates back in the wing and another goose flies point. It is sensible to take turns doing demanding jobs, whether with people or with geese flying south.

Geese honk from behind to encourage those up front to keep up their speed. What messages do we give when we honk from behind?

Finally — and this is important — when a goose gets sick or is wounded by gunshot, and falls out of formation, two other geese fall out with that goose and follow it down to lend help and protection. They stay with the fallen goose until it is able to fly or until it dies, and only then do they launch out on their own, or with another formation to catch up with their group.

If we have the sense of a goose, we will stand by each other like that.

Leadership

Sales can be solitary, but leading a sales team even more so. The temptation to be 'one of the boys' must give way to a little distance. Sometimes, standing apart takes courage.

We can easily confuse 'management' with 'leadership'. They are linked but also separate. In his book *Can You Manage?*, Ivor Kenny said on managing change, *"Job protection is at the root of all resistance to change"*.

Of course it is. Without a job, there is no income, no purpose, no joy and constant stress. Yet why is it that some people can obstruct everything?

It is always easy to know what to do, not so easy getting people to do it. Leadership starts with vision. That vision must be effectively communicated to the troops. They have to buy in or the vision will quickly turn into a ghastly nightmare.

Great managers don't necessarily make great leaders and great leaders often make terrible managers. I've met both. They can blur. Perhaps the simplest quote that articulates this is Peter Drucker's line: *"Management is doing things right; leadership is doing the right things"*.

May I add? Inevitably, doing the right thing will be the more difficult, but only you can decide.

Finally, in Ivor Kenny's *Can You Manage?*, he makes an interesting observation about leaders: *"By far the most common description is 'Tough but fair'. Nobody says 'Fair but tough'"*.

CHAPTER 14
CLOSING:
THE DRAMATIC MOMENT

Sometimes we stare so long at a door that is closing that we see too late the one that is open.
Alexander Graham Bell

I've read many books and definitions about 'closing the sale'. I don't like any of them. They are too simplistic. It's not something where you can pull out a pocket book guide to assist you.

Closing the sale is a combination of intuition, experience, skill and doing the right thing.

It's also about earning the right to do it.

Instead of the 'perfect guide to closing a sale', let me give you some thoughts to consider and a story or two. Each comes from my own adventures, mistakes and success.

First, why is it that we rush to sell and rush to close? Is it because we don't want to give the customer half a chance to criticise us or, worse still, to make some suggestions that might just accelerate our path to success?

Let me give you a simple fact. Not good, not bad, just a fact.

In our business, the most successful things that we do were not created by us; they were created by customers who gave us feedback, suggestions and ideas.

Sometimes, to learn how to close sales well, you need to screw up a few times. I did. Sometimes, with spectacular results or, should I say, with spectacular no results.

One occasion stands out. But before I tell you the story, let me plant a very simple and useful thought into your mind's toolbox. It is: *"Let's move from 'we think to 'we know"*. Or, to put it another way: *"A thought is not a fact"*. If I had been equipped with this useful piece of simple intelligence, I might have had a different result. I didn't, so I screwed up because I 'assumed'.

The Cheapest in Class

I was lucky. I was tipped off that the eminent Dublin-based architect was on his way to London to look at office interior systems for his client. With a little effort, I managed to get our company onto the shortlist.

The client was constructing a new headquarters building. The lucky office furniture contractor would win a prize worth over £1 million.

We had made it to the last four. In our heads, we had to do just two things: prepare well and then worry about how we would spend the substantial profits. Both consumed us.

"We need to be different", we all agreed.

Our West End showrooms were fantastic, the ultimate in German engineering. And, more than anything else, our product was built to the same everlasting standard as their famed World War Two tanks – bomb- and bullet-proof. This was to be our unique selling point. All it would take was a memorable demonstration of our superpower and its innate, inimitable strength.

We began to plan. I agreed to do the presentation. I would begin my short talk standing in one of the drawer pedestals. That alone would make a statement about how tough these German desks were. Rather than nice flowery paper packs, my accompanying presentation tools included a bottle of dark blue ink, a coin, a cigarette, a box of matches and a damp cloth. If nothing else, the architect would wonder what they were all about. We would stand out as I stood in.

The architect and his team arrived *en masse*. Patient and punctual, they gave us their full attention.

I began. First, I climbed into the drawer and began my talk. Their eyebrows rose in perfect harmony. Next, I continued my talk while walking across the desk. The drawer didn't break, the top didn't scratch. They didn't speak. I lit a cigarette. When it began to glow, I placed it on the desktop as nonchalantly as I could where it smouldered away. Finally, I spilt the dark blue ink across the pristine table top and invited them to scratch away with the coin. When I was finished, I used the damp cloth to sweep away every scrap of evidence of the torture we had inflicted on the desk. In seconds, it was back to new and nothing remained of the ink, coin or burns. They seemed impressed. We had made our points.

When they were gone, we were high. We knew we had made an impact, stood out and put it up to the opposition. Of course, we didn't see what we didn't see, so we were living on assumptions.

The weeks passed slowly and no phone call came to congratulate us or to tell us we had been successful. Doubt crept in. Worse, our friendly architect was in hiding.

Eventually I got him. Being a very nice man, he was full of apology. In my heart, I knew this was not the language or tone of a successful bid. He delivered the *"Thank you but no thank you"* news and our hearts collectively sank.

I needed to know why.

"It was a great presentation", began the architect. "Absolutely first class and certainly memorable. We were impressed and we were very very close to giving you the contract".

We hung on his every word, knowing that a *"but"* was on its way.

"But you made one mistake and you repeated it again and again."

My mind raced, running through a near perfect presentation. What he said next, I never anticipated.

"You kept saying that this systems furniture was the very best and the cheapest in its class."

We couldn't see what was wrong with that. Then again, we were young.

He went on: "You see, our client only ever wanted the best. You said 'cheapest'. If you had said 'dearest' you would have won. He has a problem with 'cheap' and he can afford to. I'm so sorry."

From that day to this, I have lived by the idea of "Let's move from 'we think' to 'we know'".

'Thinking' can be a very expensive luxury.

The Man in the Sauna

Julian was very British. He adored monarchy, rituals and classic English brands. His beautiful tailor-made suits matched his array of colourful club ties, even if his connection to some of them was a little vague. He had a moustache too and it was no coincidence that he was an expert on the Battle of Britain and its Spitfire pilots. Though he never said so, I'm sure this was his alter ego.

Julian was a brilliant salesman but, like the rest of us, he had flaws. His was impatience.

Julian was excited at being despatched to Finland to close a very large engineering sale. It was a chance to fly the flag. He even polished his British racing green car for the journey to Heathrow.

He was well prepared and his fine brown leather briefcase had all the papers. It was a long day but it went well. The Finns were expressionless but there were no obvious objections. At 5pm on the dot, the day ended and everything was done. But Julian hadn't inked the signature yet.

Ari was a huge man with a huge belly. He was the boss. He was a very quiet man, a great listener and the perfect poker player. He gave nothing away.

"As you are in Finland, come, meet me at 6pm in the sauna", he said to Julian.

Julian, very British Julian, was not used to such negotiating platforms. Reluctantly, he agreed, wondering whether his Union Jack swimsuit would be OK.

Nervously, Julian entered the white-hot breathless room. Spreading his huge frame and sweating from every pore, Ari was king. There was silence and it went on. For Julian, it was unbearable. He burst.

"So Ari, were you happy with our presentation, contract and price?".

"Hmmm" came Ari's reply.

Julian had no idea what this meant and quickly concluded it was negative. He pounced: "How about we forget the €1 million price tag and settle at €875,000?".

With eyes looking skyward, Ari went "Hmmm" yet again.

Julian was starting to lose the plot. Panic wasn't far away. The ambiguous utterings were far from clear. He just could not lose this sale. Everything was on the line.

"Look Ari, you're a busy man. Come on, let's get this done at €799,000 and we have a deal."

Deeply relaxed and calm, Ari sighed once more and said, "Hmmm".

Julian had enough. Standing upright far too quickly, he hit his head on the hot tin roof.

"Final, final offer, Ari. No more messing around. No games. Let's just do it. Final final final offer, €625,000."

Ari looked very slightly surprised but, with eyes closed, he was enjoying his sauna too much to flap.

Julian, his voice pitching higher in pure terror, squealed: "Have we a deal Ari, have we, have we?".

Calm as you like, Ari said, "Yes, my friend. Yes, of course. We have a deal".

Julian – weak from the sauna, the stress and the day – fell in a watery heap.

That night, in the bar, they celebrated together. Julian, now completely composed again and wearing his best cavalry twill, had a more confident, if a little curious, edge.

"You know Ari, you're one tough businessman. One tough negotiator. A tough nut and, believe me, I've mixed it with the very best of them."

A slightly bemused Ari said. "Am I? I didn't think I am like that".

"Oh yes, you are. I could read you like a book, a very complex but riveting book", said Julian, proud of how he was painting colourful pictures.

"When I played my first card, you went 'Hmmm'. It's an impressive tactic but I just knew you weren't going to buy. I quickly changed gear, upped the pace, not once but twice and read your 'Hmmm' so well. I knew, just knew I had to nail you at €625,000. If not, all over. I'd be unhappy and you too."

"Really", said Ari, intrigued by the analysis and even more intrigued by how well Julian thought he had read him. "Actually Julian, I must disagree with you."

Julian felt his nerves going and his knees weaken. *"What now?"*

"You see, my friend, when you said €1 million, I thought to myself 'Hmmm, that seems a fair price'. Then, when you went to €875,000, I said 'Hmmm' because I didn't want to interrupt you. Finally, my friend, I was just about to say 'Yes' when you said €799,000 but I couldn't interrupt you. So, we finally settled at €625,000 and I am happy."

Julian spilt his drink.

Always remember that you have two ears and one mouth. It's not a bad idea to use them in that ratio.

Seven Sharp Thoughts

First, you must earn the right to ask for the sale. Have you really done everything that was asked of you and more? If not, it's going to be your problem not theirs.

Second, patience. Sales people fire too early. Their own anxiety can overrun their emotions. Great sales people are patient, calm and listen. If you don't believe me, think of their opposites.

Third, bad sales people think it is all about money and fold instantly. It's not, it's about value, function and, more than anything else, it's about *"Does it make my life easier or better?"*.

Fourth, facts don't always matter and logic doesn't always work. People buy from people they like – whether we like it or not. However, failure will certainly come if you pretend to be the person you are not.

Fifth is trust. No sale will happen without it. If I don't trust you, I'm not giving you my money. It's as simple as that.

Sixth is about not caring. If you don't care, I don't either. Tokenism and clichés are just that. Evidence matters but without trying to prove the point.

Seventh is all about your problem. Over the years, I can tell you the thousands of times I've heard sales people utter those immortal words, *"I'm waiting for him to get back to me"*. Don't. If you wait, you'll fail. Quite simply, it's your 'problem', not his.

CHAPTER 15
AFTER THE SALE

Happiness does not come from doing easy work but from the afterglow of satisfaction that comes after the achievement of a difficult task that demanded our best.
Theodore Isaac Rubin

We can be very good at complicating simple things. Some professions have turned it into an art form and the bamboozling is designed to add mystery, intrigue and extra noughts to your invoice.

We also can be very good at making false promises in the heat of battle, just to close the sale. You know what I mean: saying *"Yes"* too quickly – or *"No problem"* too much – or *"Of course"* to almost anything. It can be the undoing of a sale – worse, it can lead to the demise of your brand.

How you communicate and sum up after a meeting gives the customer an insight into you. It tells him or her whether you listened, whether you got it and whether you are the right person to work with.

Too often, salespeople – in their haste to close – destroy themselves at the final fence. Do it right and you'll sprint away from the competition. Do it wrong and you'll hand your work to them on a golden plate.

My Dream Job

Like many people, I took wrong career turns. Sometimes, I ended up in horrid cul-de-sacs. Still, there is no job I've ever done that didn't teach me precious lessons. Always interested in understanding the anatomy of success and failure, I inadvertently fine-tuned my own skills. Not so much out of science but more out of common sense. If I saw someone skid off-track, I simply wanted to avoid the same mistake. That, inadvertently, told me what to do as well as what not to do.

Once upon a time, I hated my job. I prayed they'd fire me. They were really good people. They didn't. It was a funny conundrum.

Then I read an article on Mel McNally, founder of The Irish Pub Company: an architect, visionary and natural-born teacher. The article ticked every box on my wish list: design, travel, international, hospitality, brands and getting to work with Guinness, Ireland's most iconic brand. After reading the article, I wrote to Mel.

A week went by and no reply came. I was edging towards disappointment but 'giving up' was never an option. It was my need, not his. That was the challenge.

One day, I opened the newspaper and there, in all its glory, was a well-constructed advert for a Sales and Marketing Manager for The Irish Pub Company. I didn't know whether to laugh or cry.

The good news was that they had a need. The bad news was that everyone else would see it too. Game on.

The interview process started with 124 applicants. They were whittled down to a shortlist of 25 for interview. Over a five-month period, the list went down to five, then three, then two – and, eventually, to me.

I got the job on my birthday – the best birthday present ever.

It was a fast-moving, exciting and energetic company. I loved it. We travelled so extensively that we had our own travel agent in the office. Each day was like a lottery: *"Where to next?".* It was supercharged in every way.

One late night in New York there was just Mel and I. He was always great company. He had a huge degree of kindness and most of all, patience. He made time for you, no matter what demands were on his own shoulders. In the six years I worked for him, I learnt more from Mel than in all the earlier years of my career put together.

We got talking about how I got the job against the other people on the short list of 25 – or even the final five. Mel asked me if I knew why I got the job.

I instantly said, "Yes, I do".

He smiled and took out a $100 bill. Placing it on the table, he said, "If you're right, you keep it. If you're wrong, you owe me".

I accepted the challenge and I said just this: "The follow-up letter".

Mel smiled and pushed the $100 towards me.

You see, at my final interview with Mel, I asked him some very pointed questions. The most important one was: "What really matters to you about the person you wish to appoint?".

Mel thought it through. Slowly, he told me what he was looking for. I concentrated hard. When the interview was over, I got into my car and, as quick as I could, I wrote down the 10 points he had made. Then I went home and wrote him a letter.

To this day, I remember my letter. It went like this:

Dear Mel,
I enjoyed meeting you again today and thank you.
From our discussions, you said these were the 10 most important characteristics of the person you'd like to appoint:
(I listed the 10 points)
I look forward to our next conversation.
I will call you in the next few days.
Best wishes,
Conor

Of course, it wasn't the letter. It was what it represented.

More importantly, it was that it didn't say what every sales letter frequently says: *"I look forward to hearing from you"*. Perhaps that horrible ending is made worse by *"in due course"*?

If you want to win a sale or get your dream job, don't give up, don't wait and don't respond *"in due course"*.

Joining the Gym

I had just come home from a family holiday in Wisconsin where I had enjoyed a wonderful, happy time.

One memory stood out: our time in the log cabins at Iron River. As the name suggests, it is where real Indians live and the child within me could dream again. Bears came at night to see if we had left any treats. They knew how to make a point. If there were no treats, they clattered the bins ensuring you didn't sleep. I was surprised they didn't leave a note saying, *"Next time, or else!"*.

One morning, I got up early and headed for the sleepy lake and the little boat with the little engine. I sat silently in the middle of the sunny lake and saw a golden eagle catch breakfast. It was pure ballet. Later, I came in and fell happily asleep, tied to the sun-soaked jetty. Fast asleep, my photo was taken. A photo that, strangely enough, changed my life.

Weeks later, I discovered the undeveloped film and took it to be processed. I was looking forward to happy memories of the golden eagle and more. Instead, I got a whale, a beached whale.

"It's not me, it couldn't be. I'm not that fat."

I was. I was horrified – but the camera didn't lie.

That was many years ago and the trauma of that photo led me to a five times a week regime of running and overall healthy living. In hindsight, it was a God-sent gift. I resolved, no matter what I felt, to conquer my self-doubt, fear and embarrassment. I was going to join the gym.

The night before, I had nightmares about the athletic, toned bodies that would sneer as I waddled past. What to wear? What does one wear to a gym? I had never been.

Today is OK. It was just a meeting with the sales person. Nothing to be anxious about. A well-cut suit would disguise my not so well-cut shape.

Caroline was cheerful, chunky and energetic. Her less than perfect frame gave me some comfort. She was engaging, confident and appeared popular. I was being drawn in.

I walked the newbie gym walk in my out of sync suit. Muscly, sweating men mixed easily with perfectly-shaped and toned women. I could feel myself blushing and the fire exit was a real option. I persisted. Despite my acute lack of confidence, I liked the atmosphere. When we were done, Caroline asked me when I was planning my first visit.

I said, "Tomorrow at 8pm".

Quick as a flash, Caroline sealed the deal with these words: "That's brilliant, Conor. 8pm tomorrow is just ideal. I'll be here waiting and I'll walk you through everything".

I slept well that night, my fear virtually evaporated.

I turned up 10 minutes early the next evening. I was anxious but comforted by my 8pm appointment with Caroline. I waited and waited and waited. At 8:35pm, I was still waiting.

A very pleasant instructor, conscious of my lingering presence, made his approach: "Are you okay? Are you waiting for someone?".

Trying to look nonchalant and confident, I said: "Oh, I'm fine, I'm waiting for Caroline. I'm sure she will be here shortly".

He looked perplexed: "I think there's some confusion. Caroline only ever works until 3pm. She doesn't work Monday either. I think you must have been mistaken."

Trying to look detached, I said, "Of course, silly me. I'll be back later in the week".

I never did forget Caroline. Her face, her smiling face was forever etched on my brain. I couldn't get cross with Caroline, just myself.

Years later, I was in for another surprise. Thankfully, this time, I was more toned, less fat and much fitter. I wouldn't have blamed anyone for not recognising the old Conor in the new me.

I had been retained as the external interviewer by a large and wonderful company. It's a big brand I admire and their strong values run through every corridor. They don't talk goodness, they just do it.

A pretty cheerful girl bounded in. It was her final hurdle to a very big job. The interview went well and she was inches away from the finish. But a voice in my head couldn't come to grips with her voice. It had a distinctive tone.

Then the light dawned. It was Caroline, my dear gym person. The other interviewers were wrapping up and asked, "Conor, any more questions?".

I took up the offer and, once again, bore witness to the mesmerising smile that she knew could stun.

"Caroline, what's your view on honesty in selling?", I posed.

Caroline hit the 'play' button and gave such a compelling answer that my fellow panellists smiled.

I probed harder: "Would you ever tell a blatant lie to win a sale from an unsuspecting or vulnerable customer?" .

"Oh gosh, no, absolutely not", came the eyelid-flickering response.

My last question was "What did you say your working hours were at the gym? Was it Tuesday to Friday and from 7am to 3pm?".

Suspicious now, her guard dropped.

"Precisely" was her one-word answer – but the others had spotted the venom.

"So, you'd never ever tell a potential customer you'd meet them at – say 8am on Monday – knowing you wouldn't be there?"

Suddenly realising who I was and that there was no escape, Caroline stood up swiftly and attacked: "A company like this is not for me. Goodbye".

We looked at one another and collectively said, "She's right".

CHAPTER 16
HOW NOT TO SELL

Champions do not become champions when they win the event, but in the
hours, weeks, months and years they spend preparing for it. The victorious
performance itself is merely the demonstration of their championship character.
Alan Armstrong

In a strange way, it's easier to learn how not to sell than it is to focus on doing it right.

Being prescriptive about sales and selling doesn't work. Every situation is different and has a colourful combination of emotion, motivation and price at its core. But, sometimes, to know how to do something, you need to know what not to do.

The Sandwich-maker

Colm is a trusted advisor and a very wise man. One day, he told me a great story about his daughter. It's a simple story but, in 30 years of selling, it's one that stands out in my mind.

Every day, she headed for college with a packed lunch that her Mum had made for her. One morning, for many reasons, an under-pressure Mum let standards drop – and the resulting sandwiches were not quite to her daughter's delight. Reflecting just how well she had been raised, her response was powerful and proportionate. It teaches a great lesson about impact, behaviour and confidence. She came back from college and never said a word. No complaint, no fuss, just a normal evening. The next morning, after she had left home for her early bus, Mum noticed a piece of paper prominent on the family noticeboard.

Its heading? *"The Do's and Don'ts of Making Sandwiches."* In many ways, learning to sell is like that. As well as learning what to do, you also need to learn what not to do.

A Flashy Sports Car

It's funny how something tacky can contain great depth and great wisdom. Many years ago, some cheesy postcards grabbed my attention. They were slightly humorous, with predictable punch lines. One caught my eye and I have never forgotten the moral behind the message.

He had just picked up his brand new, red soft-top sports car. It growled and roared and he turned many heads. With a little impatience and a lack of skill, he went too fast. In seconds, his dream car was wrapped around a lamppost, destroyed. The picture showed the driver standing looking forlornly at his wrecked pride and joy, scratching his head in disbelief. The caption said it all: *"It take 3,416 bolts to hold a sports car together. It takes just one nut to dismantle them"*.

Sales is a little like that!

Watch Your Language

How we write, what we say, and the language we use, tells our audience a great deal about who we are.

Writing and talking are the two primary tools of every sales person. Use them wisely.

Think about a doctor who sends you a note full of misspelling. What does that say to you?

Imagine you are planning your wedding day at the stunning 5-star hotel but the quotation you receive is full of mistakes?

Or better still, what does the following letter tell you about a salesman who once tried to sell me a new car?

Dear Conor,
How are you, Conor?
All good in your world, Conor?
Anyway, we have a car that you're just going to love. I picked it myself.
She's a really cool monster.
Give us a call whenever you're on the loose and you can check her out.
Rob

The letter collapsed for several obvious reasons. You can choose yourself whether or not you'd buy a car from Rob.

The enemy of good writing is the belief that you have conveyed your message. Often, we haven't.

Of course, we might know what we are saying or at least, want to say, but it is folly to assume we got the right message across to our potential customer.

Good communication means I ought to 'understand' what you said. Anything else is just ribbons and curls.

"I Can't Remember His Other Name"

Everybody has become a reporter. What was once hidden in a deep drawer can now take flight in minutes. The online world has given voice where there was none and given speed that was unthinkable in the past. Like a sharp knife, it's double-edged.

Of course, life would be great if we were all perfect – but we are not. Sometimes, emotions run riot over logic and common-sense. The problem is that the Internet never forgets when these things happen. TripAdvisor is a bible for most of today's online travellers. Some like it, some don't. Some trust it, some don't. Regardless, it is visited every second. If something is on TripAdvisor and you're reading it, so are your customers.

A friend forwarded a copy of a complaint on TripAdvisor about a hotel we both knew well. He sent it to a lot of people. I read it in disbelief.

The customer's complaint seemed fair and reasonable: there was no hot water, the heating didn't work … that kind of complaint. It followed a logic and it was factual, without emotion. Towards the end of his well-crafted account, the customer recounted how he had sought out the manager.

Summoned, the manager was not happy but made a superficial kind of response that resolved the situation. The complainant decided to stand down. The manager had other ideas.

You see, the complainant couldn't remember the manager's name. He knew his first name but not his surname. In his lengthy complaint, he referred to the manager as *"Frank I can't remember his other name"*. For sure, it wasn't a warm friendly term.

But the response was volcanic. When the manager ended his online response, how did he sign himself? You got it :*"Frank I can't remember his other name – The Manager"*.

Yes indeed, the Internet never forgets and bad customer relations can go viral in a way you wouldn't like. Be careful what you say, when you say it and how you say it. Some momentary ego-boosting moments can lead to a lifetime of memories that you probably wouldn't want.

The Worst Salesman Ever

Most evenings when we get home, we walk over the thin pile of promotional leaflets dropped daily through our letterbox. They can be annoying but, now and again, they might just be the right message at the right time.

A house, just like a business, needs constant maintenance, upgrading and investment. In my case, it was time to spend a little. The leaflet was very well constructed. It had thought through all the questions a noise-conscious, security-conscious and heat loss-conscious customer might want. Forget double glazing and think treble glazing. The leaflet captured my attention. I put it aside, Monday would do.

On Monday, I called the office. More excellence. A cheery girl could not have been better.

"When would suit you for us to call?", she asked.

I asked if 8pm was OK.

Cheerfully she said it was perfect. I was halfway to buying already.

It was a beautiful summer's evening and still broad daylight at 8pm. Right on time, Mr Salesman arrived. His tiny bit of tyre squealing heralded an over-eager appointment – or so I thought. Never mind, top marks for being on time. I waited at my front door as he ran – literally ran – the few short yards to it. His speed was dazzling. Breathless, he came within three inches of my face. The ill-fitting suit and skewed, stained tie diminished my former confidence. His next line is forever etched in my mind. No introduction, no greeting, no *"May I?"*, no nothing.

Instead, he said, "I need to use your bathroom - now".

When his emergency was over, I couldn't quite bring myself to shake hands now that he was introducing himself – from inside my house. He didn't make a sale that day but he certainly achieved one thing: he stood out from the crowd – but for all the wrong reasons.

"I'm In Such a Dark Place"

Almost nobody rings my dust-gathering landline, which remains parked on my desk like some ode to the past. It's there because it's there. One early autumn night, at 9pm, I was deep into writing and even deeper into my train of thought.

The shrill ring of the telephone startled me. I almost leapt from my chair. I wondered who on earth might be calling this technological dinosaur. Warily, I answered the call.

In a deep South American accent, I got this: "Hey, Good morning, Kenny O'Connor. How are you this sunny morning?".

I was not Kenny, O'Connor, in the morning, or in the sunshine. However, I was touched by his concern for my wellbeing.

I was also curious and, knowing he was using a well-rehearsed script, I decided, a little unfairly, to test his agility beyond the script.

"Thank you, thank you, I'm very grateful", I said in my most sincere tone.

I knew I had thrown him because his best offering was "Sorry, Kenny, whadya mean?".

I pushed a little further: "I just wanted to thank you so much for asking me how I am. It's kind of you and so very caring but, to be honest, I'm in a very dark place. I've lost my job, lost my friends, lost my mind and at least you care. Thank you for asking me how I am today. It means so much".

He hung up. So did I.

Failing to sell is soul-destroying. The good news is that it is easily corrected. Great sales are all about relationships but beware of how fragile they can be.

CHAPTER 17
GREAT SALES PEOPLE

The difference between a successful person and others is not a lack of strength, not a lack of knowledge, but rather a lack of will.

Vince Lombardi

There is only so much you can put in one book about selling and only so many Sales Tales that make sense. Perhaps the important question is *"What do great sales people have in common?"*.

Of course, I don't have the answer – though I do know some common threads that I've seen over and over.

But first, some stories.

Liam Healy

I came out of university with a very average degree and an above average attitude. My college scarf was a badge of honour – I think I even wore it to bed. It was my way of saying *"Look at me, aren't I great?"*. I wasn't. I was average, nothing more.

I sent my résumé flying in every direction. Supermarkets, design companies, a joinery – anyone that might give me a job. But I didn't really want their job. I just wanted the money that a job would bring.

Selling myself was a steep learning curve. Compared to all the other graduates, my only point of difference was that I was me. With youthful confidence, I knew I needed a big reference given that I'd accomplished almost nothing. After all, winning a school bicycle race, aged 10, was not a great indicator of anything to come.

Liam Healy was a family friend. He also ran a global newspaper empire – he was at the very top of a very big tree. He was also unassuming, a gentleman and knew all about doing the 'right thing'. All he needed to do was to respond to my letter, giving me permission to use his name as a reference. That would do it, easy. Not for Liam Healy. He didn't do easy, he did the right thing.

A beautiful letter came back. It was handwritten. Before he would give me a reference, he wanted to meet me, spend time understanding me and just guiding me. I was surprised and impressed. I called his secretary and found she shared his values too.

"What time would suit you, Conor?", she asked politely.

What time would suit me? Me? I was unemployed and had all God's time. That struck me too.

We agreed a 10am slot. I arrived on time.

In the waiting room, I began to see the enormity of this busy empire and realised that I was about to meet the man at the very top. I got nervous.

At 10am precisely, Liam came towards me with outstretched hand and a welcoming smile. I never forgot his very first words.

"How are you for time, Conor?"

I think that says it all.

John Condon

Twenty years ago, I saw someone take a big risk and trust his own judgement. John Condon had been working in Louis Copeland's fine men's shop since I first entered its hallowed ground. It's a shop with a fine tradition and an enviable reputation. Rarely, in my career, have I experienced excellence with such consistency over so long. Instinctively, they just do it right. That comes from the top.

My boss at the time was a regular customer. He dressed beautifully and always came to work in suits I really coveted. Through him, I had admired their store for a long time. It was easy to spot their suits on perfectly polished gentlemen. Not only did I admire them, I envied them. Like all young men aspiring to be well-dressed and dapper, this was a step too far for a poor professional.

"One day", I promised myself.

To visit this store with a very tight budget was scarier than going to the dentist for an extraction. Would they ask me to leave? Would they scoff at my youth? Would they fall about laughing when I told them my tragically poor budget? What on earth was I thinking even drifting in their direction? Curiosity, got the better of me. I was feeling the fear but doing it anyway.

The door opened before I could answer my own questions. Coming out was my favourite boss of all time. Far from using the moment to bask in his own glory, he immediately turned to a young man called John Condon: "This is one of my men, John, make sure you look after him".

John welcomed me in. He would have anyway.

It was the cathedral of sartorial suits. I was mesmerised. My budget of £200 was not just non-negotiable, it was already creaking, screaming and groaning. Ambling around, to my horror, I saw an 'ordinary' suit with a price tag of £450. I was doomed. Now, all my energy and focus went into planning a hasty and blushing retreat.

John spotted my distress. Gently, he worked his magic.

"Now", he said. "Just forget all about those prices and tell me why you came in".

I mumbled something about a grey pin-striped suit but quickly said: "It's fine, don't worry, I'm way out of my depth. I can't see anything that I like, I'll go now".

John, with true humility, wasn't going to let me down. In a way, he admired my naivety and innocent courage. Eventually, he persuaded me to describe my dream suit.

"Wait there", said John. I was too confused to defy him.

Minutes later, he appeared with the most beautiful suit I had ever seen. The detail, the hand-stitching, the cloth and then, the price tag. I could feel my knees turn to rubber. It was £850. Handing the suit back, I said, "I couldn't afford a leg, let alone the whole suit".

"How much have you to spend?", John enquired.

With red cheeks getting redder, I said, "£200".

What he said next came out of the blue but John was using his finely-tuned judgement.

"Try it on. Don't worry, I'm not going to sell it to you. I just want to see the fit".

I did. It was perfect. Proudly, I came out to show him.

"It's yours now", said John. "You can have it for £200."

I was stunned. After all, this was the kind of suit I dreamed of wearing one day. That day was certainly not this particular day. Or so I thought.

I asked him why he would do such a thing and this is what John said: "It was ordered by someone your size who subsequently cancelled it after his business got into trouble. Take it, it's yours. It's not often a tailor-made order fits someone else perfectly".

Twenty years on, and I don't know how many suits later, I still buy my suits from John. I won't be changing anytime soon. Not only did John have great judgement, he made a customer for life and we still share the story every time we meet.

Guinness Is Good For You

Some years back, I had the great pleasure of working with Ireland's most iconic brand, Guinness. It was a very happy time and a university of exceptional experience. Much learning, many memories and, above all, passionate, loyal people. They believed in their company, their brand and, most importantly, their values. Whether I was on the west coast of the USA or in Slovenia, every time I worked with Guinness people there was absolute consistency. First and foremost, that's what a brand is all about.

John Mullins was my daily Guinness business contact. John is Guinness through and through. John loves Guinness and Guinness loves John. It has been a lifelong love affair from the age of 16. Although he 'retired' many years ago, he still has not left.

I travelled with John many times and his innate charisma, authenticity and razor-sharp mind taught me lessons that I still use today. Passion ran through everything John did. It is infectious and, most of all, it builds confidence. For me, in a long career, John stands out as one of the greatest influences on my journey and really understanding how to sell.

A man from Spain wanted to build an Irish pub back home. He came to the brewery at St. James' Gate. John was representing Guinness and I was representing The Irish Pub Company.

The man hummed and hawed and price kept derailing his thinking. He was a nice man and didn't want to offend. Eventually, he came out with it: "But if I build this pub in Spain, with local craftsmen, I will save myself €30,000".

My heart sank. At last, the truth was coming out, the sale was doomed. Not for John Mullins.

Quick as a flash, John looked him in the eye and, in a solemn voice said: "That would be the most expensive €30,000 you ever saved".

Our Spanish guest paused with a jaw inclined towards the floor. In broken English, he replied: "Okay, we go ahead".

A unique combination of charisma, character and authentic confidence, coupled with strong beliefs and doing the right thing, brought a sale back from the dead.

Now you can see why Guinness won't let John go. Of course, they are right.

The Greatest

Of course, great sales people are not just great sales people, they are simply great people who are in sales.

Over many years, I have learnt by listening, observing and by looking at what people did that had a good impact on me. The list below is not scientific, it's just my view and my perspective on what makes great sales people great:

- **Humility:** Great sales people are humble. They never let their ego get in the way.
- **Trust:** You trust them instinctively. They have earned that.
- **See good:** They focus on the good, not the weakness. They forgive customers who are difficult.
- **Positive:** 'Cheerful' and 'positive' are among the words that describe the most successful sales people. The opposite isn't very inviting.

- **Honest:** They are honest – always.
- **What's right:** They will only do what is right for their customer, even when that means saying *"No"*.
- **Knowledge:** They know what they sell and how it benefits their customer.
- **Confident:** Confidence is essential in selling and great sales people are only confident because they believe in their proposition.
- **Learn:** They have a desire to learn throughout their career.
- **Judge:** They don't. They listen and welcome alternative perspectives.
- **Curious:** They have a natural curiosity and an innate ability to question.
- **People:** They simply love being around, and with, people.
- **Fast:** They are driven by fixing problems – and fixing them quickly too.
- **Brand:** They know their brand, its behaviour, culture and personality.
- **Personality:** They are who they are and never try to be someone else.
- **Listen:** They are good listeners above all else.
- **Promises:** They are passionate about delivering what they promised.
- **Value:** They like to add value, which usually means effort.
- **Work hard:** They work hard and usually longer hours than their contract requires.
- **Shortcuts:** They don't take them.
- **Accessible:** Great sales people don't turn off their phone.
- **Balance:** They understand the importance of not working every hour.
- **Fair:** They understand a good deal must be a good deal for both parties.

- **Say "No":** They know when to say *"No"* – when it's a bad deal for the customer.
- **Winning:** They don't see a good deal as a win – they see it as a draw.
- **Persistent:** They don't quit, even when they're told to.
- **Standards:** They have high standards in every part of their life.
- **Emotions:** They rarely let them get in the way.
- **Focus:** They keep their eye on the goal, not the journey.
- **Rejection:** They don't allow rejection to interfere with their goal.
- **Energetic:** They move fast, not slow.
- **Character:** They have charisma, even if they don't believe it themselves.

Another way to see the qualities of great sales people is to pause for one moment and think about the sales people you have met who really impressed you. You will find that the characteristics you admire and trust are all within the list above. We don't often sit back and analyse these traits but they exist, they work and they're the DNA of really good sales people.

Above all else, the key quality of a great sales person is that you trust them. If you don't, nothing else will happen.

AFTERWORD

We begin our careers in childhood, we just don't realise it. It's then the mould is made and we become who we are. Sometimes, becoming – or even discovering – who you are is difficult, cloudy and confusing. I know, I was there.

If you do what you are, you will succeed.

If you are what you do, you will succeed.

If you set out to sell in the hope that it will lead to the job that you actually want, you will miss the present.

If you miss the present, you live in one of only two imaginary places: the future or the past – neither are real, they exist only in our mind.

Talk to children. They have no interest in the past or the future. They focus on now. Look at how happy they are. They are living, whilst we grown-ups are planning. We have much to learn from children and their appreciation for now.

For me, there is NO difference between who I am and what I do. It certainly wasn't always so.

It takes time to find your path and time to find your way. When you do, you begin to see how all the wrong turns brought you to this very moment. Remember, your story – your journey – is not who you are. It's just that: your story – and it got you to here.

Great sales people – great *anything* people – are happy people. They are happy because they understand how useless it is to live anywhere other than in the now. They enjoy the beauty of each day, each challenge and each moment. It's what every one of us should aspire to – and, if we can't, we are probably in the wrong job.

My Dad is a beautiful writer. He has a gift for saying important things in few words. I say what I want to say by telling stories and by painting pictures. You must communicate in your own way.

When I set out to write this book, I realised I didn't know how to write a book. That didn't stop me. I wrote it my way. It's neither right, nor wrong; it's just my way. Whatever you do, in life, in work or in sales, do it your way. That's what makes you memorable, special and not one of the crowd. You are who you are.

Finally, I'm going to use family privilege and steal the last word from my Dad's book, *Can You Manage?*. Not because it is his book but because, like all simple and deep lines, it had a huge impact when I read it first. It still does now.

I hope it will guide you in sales, in your career and in life.

It's not what's ahead – today is the golden time.

CONOR KENNY
& ASSOCIATES

Conor Kenny & Associates are a training, mentoring, learning and professional development company.

Our work, focus and passion is growing people and business for hotel, hospitality and service sector companies.

Our primary skills are people development, professional development, sales & marketing, HR and growing the talent and opportunities within.

Everything we do is practical, measurable, actionable, effective and intelligent.

So, if you want to make something happen for you, your people or your business, come on in, have a look around, see who we work with, and the many ways we can help you grow.

It's not just what we do, it's the way that we do it.

CONOR KENNY

Conor is the Founder and Principal of Conor Kenny & Associates, Ireland's leading independent training, mentoring, HR, learning and professional development company for the hospitality industry.

His skill is teaching and training the art of sales, marketing and business and growing talent. An advisor and mentor to several private and State companies, Conor is a columnist for the UK's hotel industry magazine. His view has been widely sought by the BBC (TV), Jools Holland (TV), BBC Scotland (TV), BBC (Radio), Sky (TV), RTÉ (TV), RTÉ (Radio), Newstalk (Radio), *USA Today*, *The Sunday Times*, *The Irish Times*, *The Sunday Business Post*, *The Irish Independent* and more. He is a syndicated writer for many global websites, including Cornell University and a regular contributor to business publications at home and abroad.

An expert communicator and strategist, Conor is a much in demand workshop facilitator where he guides businesses and people towards their strengths and is highly skilled at getting the best out of people.

His career started at Kilkenny Design and before Conor Kenny & Associates, he was Group Commercial Director for the Irish Pub Company, which designed and built Irish pubs in more than 70 countries. He has worked with many of the world's leading brands: Baileys, Guinness, Hennessy and Smirnoff, and international hotel groups and casino groups in Las Vegas have called on him.

In 2002 he founded Conor Kenny & Associates. Today, he and his team of specialists have over 200 Clients.

A passionate teacher and motivator, Conor is a frequent conference speaker, nationally and internationally, and has written key speeches for industry leaders.

Conor's years of experience are also employed to help advocate the charities he and his company work for.

Conor was educated at University College Dublin and the University of Greenwich, London.

A keen marathon runner, he also loves writing his award-winning blog.

OAK TREE PRESS

Oak Tree Press develops and delivers information, advice and resources for entrepreneurs and managers. It is Ireland's leading business book publisher, with an unrivalled reputation for quality titles across business, management, HR, law, marketing and enterprise topics. NuBooks is its recently-launched imprint, publishing short, focused ebooks for busy entrepreneurs and managers.

In addition, Oak Tree Press occupies a unique position in start-up and small business support in Ireland through its standard-setting titles, as well training courses, mentoring and advisory services.

Oak Tree Press is comfortable across a range of communication media – print, web and training, focusing always on the effective communication of business information.

Oak Tree Press, 19 Rutland Street, Cork, Ireland.
T: + 353 21 4313855 F: + 353 21 4313496.
E: info@oaktreepress.com
W: www.oaktreepress.com / www.SuccessStore.com.

Lightning Source UK Ltd.
Milton Keynes UK
UKOW04n1851180414

230233UK00001B/1/P